"I've Asked Miller To Say a Few Words"

"Knowing I was speaking today, Gladys said, 'Hang in there' and that's exactly what I'm going to do!!!"

"I've Asked Miller To Say A Few Words"

*New and Exciting Ways to Improve
Speaking and Presentation Skills
Through the Use of
Improvisational Comedy Techniques*

by Cherie Kerr

Foreword by Phil Hartman

Illustrations by Sam Middleton

ExecuProv Press

Printed in the United States of America

Second Edition

ISBN# 0-9648882-1-1

To

- Seanie Bird — for coming home
- Nan-Heart-One — for her strength and beauty; for her unparalleled perfection and for *always* being there
- That Donut — for his joy and bounce

And

- Donna, Keith and Cameron

For

- My mother — whose fire continues to ignite me

ACKNOWLEDGMENTS

There are so many who made this book possible and I wish to acknowledge and thank them here: Gus Lee, who encouraged me despite the obstacles; Gary T. for finding a way; Sim for not throwing his stuff away; Jane Dystel and Jim Charlton, who believed in it anyway; Tom Maxwell for his support from the beginning; Shirley Prestia, Dick Frattali, and Cathy Shambley for proving the theory; Phil Hartman for his encouragement and contribution; Gary Austin for teaching me so much; Tracy Newman for her influence; Judy Capozzola for being my S.B.F. forever; Barb for always making me feel smarter than I am; those who helped to shape me — Joe Martin especially; my wonderful clients and students (too many to mention) for giving me the privilege of working with them; the L. A. Groundlings for giving me a start; the Orange County Crazies for making me stretch and proving myself to myself; LizAnne for giving my creations a voice; my high school junior lit teacher - Miss Davis; Carol Lombard for setting an example; Eleanor Dopp for launching me; Rowena and Monina for their friendship; Audrey for her guidance; Masha, wherever the hell she is; Alex for his wisdom; Eric for his hard work and dedication to the project; Linda McNamar and Dr. Peggy Bassett for their inspiration; Sharon Connelly for her wonderful assistance; Don Cribb for his generous support; the Apollo 13 crew and Christopher Reeve for showing me and the rest of the world what balls really are; my father for his brilliance, his music, and perfection; Heather, my little big sis, lus ya buns...

A very special thanks to Drake for helping me finish this book

TABLE OF CONTENTS

FOREWORD

by Phil Hartman

I've always believed that the art of improvisational comedy was an all encompassing creative science that had more application than simply providing actors a no-holds-barred playground in which to express their at-the-moment mania. I've believed it could go beyond the thespian and out into the world to do wonders for others. It's therapeutic — it's applied psychology — it's mind expanding. We could teach the art to children to help them gain confidence. Instruct families in it to make them better communicators with one another. Give it to educators so they might be more captivating. And, of course, teach it to business professionals to make them more interesting. I can imagine what good improv comedy training can bring to the *bored* rooms of corporate America.

It makes perfect sense to arm business professionals with improv comedy instruction. Most of them are selling something. Improv comedy skills have so much to do with focus, spontaneity, problem solving and the magic of being oneself when the pressure's on. Face it, many an exec bears the big "E", scarlet letter of ennui, because they're tedious to listen to, slow or inappropriate to respond, and lack any kind of luster before any kind of audience.

When I first met the author — a fellow L.A. Groundling

(though her era preceded mine) — and she told me about her crusade of taking improv comedy techniques into the workplace through her innovative workshop series called ExecuProv, I knew it made perfect sense. Cherie's program puts business people through mental bootcamp. They come out strong, ready, proud, bright, shiny, and ever prepared for the battleground of the highly competitive business world. They can march into the front lines of any situation and win. And it's a total blast!

Once an ardent teacher of improv myself, I can see the value of introducing the "non-actor" to the same principles learned by the improv comedy student. I can see that given the opportunity to grasp such unique fundamentals, a whole new sense of self can be discovered and re-discovered.

I'm impressed with how well Kerr has integrated our improv comedy concepts into the business community. I know what a task it has been. I know what a capable teacher she is. And, I'm grateful that she cared enough to take the time to share such valuable information and compile it into a book everyone will get something from.

No matter how many public speaking books you've read, no matter how many tips you've gotten on how to put yourself out there, this book offers a whole new slant on the subject. So put that briefcase down, loosen your tie or kick off those heels, and let go...

Phil Hartman, performer and writer (NBC "Saturday Night Live" for seven seasons) and the co-star of the NBC hit sitcom, NEWSRADIO, was also a member of the famed L.A. Groundlings

*"Performing? HMMM… It looked so much easier
when I was in the audience."*

Everyone is a performer but few
people are trained to be.

— *The "Miller" Credo*

I want my Maaaaaaaawwwwmmmm??!!!!

Introduction

THE "MILLER" SYNDROME

Has this ever happened to you? Picture this: It's 7:30 A.M. or P.M.; it doesn't matter. You're seated at one of those round tables close to the front of the hotel banquet room (or maybe you're seated on the side), and it's almost time. You know that because the other attendees are finishing dessert or that second cup of coffee. You keep reading the place card in front of you.

You want to change your name.

You have maybe four, five minutes. Your breathing quickens, becomes labored. Your hands and feet begin to tingle, twitch, perspire, or go numb. There's something weird going on with your pupils. You know that because your eyes are dry, as dry as your mouth. You don't want to talk to that person who is chattering incessantly — strictly a one-sided conversation. You want to look away. To collect yourself. To look down for a moment. But when you do, all you see is one of those dizzying banquet room carpets. You feel carsick. It's almost your turn to go to the podium and speak.

Someone calls your name. You rise. It feels like slow motion as you take those few steps to get to where you know you have to go. The symptoms increase now. You're shaking. Your pulse is pounding. You're not sure, but your head might just catapult right off your neck and stick to the chandelier. You smile at the audience. Weakly. You try harder. Your upper lip sticks to your

1

front teeth. You're feeling kind of light-headed now. Limbs are jello-like. You pull out your notes. They're all mixed up. At that moment, time stands still. Everything freezes. So do you.

You want only one thing: your mother.

You don't want to continue. You have to, though.

Sound familiar? It's no big deal. It's called the "Miller" Syndrome. In one form or another, it strikes most people who don't want to speak in front of others. It also happens, to some degree, to people who do enjoy public speaking. (Incidentally, you won't die from the "Miller" Syndrome, though some of you wish you could — instantly.)

The "Miller" Syndrome is a condition that repeats itself every time you're in the same situation: WHEN YOU HAVE TO SPEAK! And, let's face it, speaking can be scary, nerve-wracking. It doesn't have to be in one of those hotel banquet rooms either. It can happen anywhere — a client's office, your office, at one of those presentations...

Speech, presentation. What's the difference? Getting up in front of people is getting up in front of people, and maybe you just don't like it. Or if you sort of do, you're not entirely comfortable.

I've Asked Miller To Say A Few Words is designed to rid you of the "Miller" Syndrome. It's a manual that will help you to understand and overcome many of the above-mentioned "symptoms" in a fun and positive way. But that's just the beginning; this book will do much more. It will train you to train yourself so that when you're called upon to make a speech or give a presentation, you'll actually enjoy it. And if you enjoy something, it's usually because you're doing it well. So sit back, relax, and get ready to have your mind take off to places it's never been before.

Chapter 1

"MILLER'S" BIRTH

I've Asked Miller To Say A Few Words is not your typical "how to speak and make presentations" book. It arises instead from a sense of theater — a rather irreverent sense of theater, to be sure — that of improvisational comedy. As a result, the techniques and approaches outlined in this book are likely to be quite different from anything you've encountered in previous attempts to become a better speaker or presenter.

Think of it this way: You like to try new things, right? Remember the first time you tried quiche. "What the hell is it?", you thought silently. Well, that same question might be popping into your mind right now as you're reading this sentence. And to tell you the truth, this book is a lot like that first quizzical quiche sensation: It looks weird, but it really isn't. After you get into it, you'll probably be pleasantly surprised at how much you like it. At least, that's been the response of participants in the many ExecuProv workshops I've conducted over the last several years. (The key words here are "executive" and "improvisation," but I'm sure you've already figured that out.)

The ideas and exercises presented in subsequent chapters provide you with an actual do-it-yourself seminar/workshop program that combines basic acting skills with the fundamental techniques of improvisational comedy training. According to the hundreds of individuals who have previously learned —

and implemented — this material, the end result can be truly phenomenal. So not only will you be enjoying yourself while you're learning the techniques, but there's likely to be a big payoff later on, in terms of speaking easily and spontaneously in front of others, and putting more interest into your "art," so to speak.

The birth of the "Miller" concept is worth mentioning. In 1972, I was a founding member of the L.A. Groundlings, an improvisational comedy organization that now enjoys a national reputation for excellence. The group has spawned a long list of celebrities, including Cassandra Peterson (aka Elvira, "Mistress of the Dark"), Pat Morita, Paul Reubens (aka Pee Wee Herman), Tim Matheson, Edie McClurg, Laraine Newman, Jon Lovitz, Julia Sweeney, and Phil Hartman — the latter four have all appeared as regulars on NBC's *Saturday Night Live*. In addition, many former members of the Groundlings have gone on to become major forces in the entertainment industry as writers, agents, directors, and so on.

As Tom Maxwell, the former artistic director of the Groundlings (who left after 15 years for a major writing contract with Disney) pointed out recently, it's impossible to find anything in entertainment today without a former Groundling attached to it in some way. They're either starring in it, writing it, scoring the music, putting the deal together, creating the idea, directing it, producing it, etc. The point is, for those who were with the Groundlings long enough, the training they received there played a crucial role in their subsequent successes. I'm certainly grateful to be one of the lucky ones in that category.

The Groundlings school is a tough one, and not everyone gets in. Once in, not everyone has what it takes to climb through the ranks and become a full-fledged Groundlings performer. Even though I studied acting as a child and received a great deal of training, what I learned from studying and performing with the Groundlings was invaluable to me. It still is.

After leaving the Groundlings, I taught improv comedy, mostly to children. In the summer of 1985 I began teaching the art of improv to members of the business community. This came about by accident. I was running my own public relations agency and occasionally accompanied my clients — mostly men and mostly entrepreneurs — to interviews on radio and television talk shows, print interviews, and press conferences. Oftentimes, I just want along with them when they had to do their thing. Most of these individuals were very successful business people working for big-name corporations. And, oh-my-god, watching them during those interviews was like watching one of your kids during their first stage performance when he or she tripped and fell (usually on a number of other children) and ruined the show. You didn't know whether to laugh or cry. (As a mother of three, I've done both in those instances — simultaneously. Many of my clients have, too, after their respective appearances.) It was sad to see these highly successful people making fools of themselves. I felt as sorry for them as I did for my clumsy children. In business they had done great; "on stage," though, they had bombed.

Numerous factors contributed to these poor performances: lack of energy; faces devoid of expression; mumbled or garbled words; monotonic voices; body language out of sync with the verbal text. The most horrifying moments for me, however, came when these otherwise accomplished business execs displayed, with metronome-like precision, their personal repertoires of nervous tics. These included — but weren't limited to — rubbing their noses, flipping their ties, teetering on tiptoe, pulling their collars away from their necks (invariably accompanied by a pained expression around the mouth), and constantly clearing their throats. All of these tics were executed as if on cue or as part of the "script."

Many times, my clients embarrassed themselves terribly, sometimes unknowingly — until they saw the video replay, that is. My vote for most "embarrassing client moment" came down to a near-tie between the uncontrollable giggle emitted by a female attorney who was asked, on a national news program, to discuss her stand on abortion, and the man who picked his nose. (You're probably thinking that the nose picker won, but since that egregious act occurred during a commercial break and was witnessed by the host and studio audience only, I voted for the giggler.)

Compounding the boredom, tics, and otherwise embarrassing actions was the fact that most of the time my clients were frightened and nervous, which made their "presentations" even worse — worse because the fear and anxiety *always* showed. Many times after their "moment" was over, they died, and I died with them. Often, the greatest horror for both of us came when they were asked impromptu questions. They simply froze; I simply freaked.

On one of those "Oh, God! Why-am-I-doing-this-for-a- living" (PR, that is) days, it suddenly struck me that maybe there was something I could do to prepare my clients for these "encounters." I began to play with the idea that by putting them through the rigors of improv comedy training, I could perhaps teach them a new way of presenting themselves, so they'd look good and feel proud. (And then maybe I'd be able to come out from hiding behind my clipboard!)

At first it was a funny, fleeting thought — the kind you get when you drive by a bank and think about robbing it. To envision grown business people in suits and ties acting out movies in three minutes, making up poems from audience suggestions, and eating nonexistent bowls of spaghetti — not to mention the countless other improv exercises I'd done for years with my students — was I nuts? Maybe. It was like trying to envision Queen Elizabeth doing the opening monologue for *The Tonight Show*. The concept seemed justifiably incongruent.

After further thought, however, I went to work on a pilot program. I brought together business executives who didn't much care for doing the public speaking thing, and put these "students" through a series of improv comedy exercises, beginning with some of the fundamentals like lessening inhibitions and speeding up mental responses. They loved them. I loved *them*. The results blew us away.

I then took each of my clients, one at a time, and videotaped segments of their speeches. I treated them much the same as a director does an actor, frequently stopping them to suggest attitude adjustments, physical changes, and other "tricks" and "secrets" that could be incorporated into their new presentation style. I'd then go through my notes with them, and we'd look at the video playback to monitor their progress. We'd add more changes. Ultimately, they were pleased; I was thrilled. During each subsequent session I would add a few more positive qualities ("We're playing Mr. Potato Head," I'd reassure them) until finally we had produced an interesting, confident, and polished "character." Through this process, my clients had become their best!

The pilot program was a big hit — a win for everyone! Since that time, all of us involved in teaching ExecuProv have come to believe that everyone in the business world should have the benefit of these workshops. Knowing that isn't necessarily realistic or possible, I did the next best thing; I did what so many other people do: I wrote a book. The "Miller" book.

No matter what kind of speaker or presenter you are, no matter how good you are already, I think this book will be of help to you, and add even more to your current abilities as a speaker.

Chapter 2

THE "MILLER" PHILOSOPHY

Here's the "Miller" philosophy in a soundbite: "Everybody's a performer, but few people are trained to be." In my view, this lack of training is a problem; and I'll tell you why.

You see, I believe that each of us is selling something — a product, a service, a philosophy, an idea. Mostly, though, what we're selling is *ourselves*. And in order to do that, in order to sell anything, we must first establish a connection with our audience, be it one or 1,000. In other words, the HUMAN CONNECTION comes first, and the sale follows from that. No connection, no sale. To put it another way: People buy people; then they buy things. Unfortunately, very few people are taught *how* to make the human connection. As a result, they may end up alienating themselves from their audiences — often when they're trying hardest to make contact.

The philosophy behind this book is that each and every business professional CAN be at his or her best as a speaker, presenter and/or communicator under any and all circumstances. And they needn't be theatrically inclined to play the game the "Miller" way — just open and receptive to new ways of putting themselves out there.

The bottom line is, if all business professionals had the "inside edge" that trained professionals do, they'd consistently outdo their competitors. I'm not referring solely to basic theatrics now, but also to a more accelerated set of techniques unique to improv comedy training. These techniques are demanding and highly advanced skills — think of them as "mental aerobics" — that change the speed and productivity of the mind. After using them for a while, people become more dynamic, confident, and interesting. Even better, they become highly spontaneous. It's through our individual, uniquely singular sense of spontaneity that *we're at our best*. And when we're at our best, we're like a positive magnet: Everything good comes our way and sticks to us.

The goal of the ExecuProv program, then, is to assist you, the business professional, in becoming the best that you can be as a speaker, presenter and/or communicator. What's the strategy here?

Well, the "Miller" approach begins with the basics, including proper breathing techniques and diction training. A few fundamental principles of acting are also discussed. There are several valuable chapters devoted to such important areas as how to deepen and intensify concentration levels, how to sharpen awareness, and how to develop and maintain a strong energy base. (Don't you hate to spend time with people who have no energy? I mean, their eyes are open, but where in the hell are they? I sometimes have the urge to slap them into liveliness.) Oh, yes, energy is critical to putting yourself across, so I'll talk a lot about that.

Additional chapters focus on self-expression and the uniqueness of each person's style of delivery. The magic of timing and tips on how to discover your own are also discussed. Since I'm a firm believer in the importance of really listening when others are speaking, there's an entire chapter devoted to the art of listening. You won't believe the difference when you learn to listen the "Miller" way.

Most of these pages will take you on a mental agility roller coaster. One of the best parts is that you'll get to explore the real miracle of imagination. Yours.

As you can see, being a "Miller" trainee is a very educational experience. But even better, it's also a lot of fun. (Contrary to my parochial school upbringing, I think the more fun you're having, the more you'll learn!) At the end of each chapter, you'll find unique and interesting exercises, so you'll be able to participate all along the way. I guarantee that this "homework" isn't tedious or laborious. In fact, it's great fun, and you can do it at your own pace. So *relax*, but be sure to practice and apply what you've learned.

The best news is that if you practice these new techniques *repeatedly*, they'll become second nature to you. You'll do them automatically, without thinking about them. It's the same idea as putting on your shoes, writing a check, opening the refrigerator, etc. When was the last time you had to actively think about how to do those things? You just did them. That's what the "Miller" process will train you to do — to respond automatically, naturally, appropriately, and best of all, *spontaneously*. In fact, as you continue to practice the "Miller" techniques, you'll find that you'll *think* less and *be* more. (By the way, therein lies the source of your charisma. But more on that later.)

What's been mentioned so far isn't *all* I have in store for you, though. Once you've conquered the basics, you'll begin to examine the "how-to's" of incorporating humor into your presentations. (In a later chapter, I dissect humor and explain its components. And by the way, I truly believe EVERYONE is funny.) You'll also get to frolic in the speech/presentation preparation game, too. There I'll illustrate how to quickly, efficiently prepare and organize a talk in just a few minutes. Come on; you can't fool me or "Miller." How often do you memorize your "script" before that *big* moment?

If you're still a little skeptical about how the "Miller" philosophy works, ask yourself this question: "How much of my day today was totally scripted? How much of it was improvised?"

Are you ready? Here we go!

Chapter 3

WHO ARE YOU "DOING"

AND IS IT GETTING YOU WHAT YOU WANT?
(The Human Connection Is the Only Connection)

I deal with individuals in a professional atmosphere every day, and in the process often ask myself: "What are they *really* like?" You see, for the most part, people have a personal demeanor, and then they have a business demeanor. And, oh, what a difference between the two!

Now, I'm not suggesting that everyone becomes a different person in the work environment. But when it comes time for that first meeting, the important presentation, the really big speech, or dealings with that all-important business associate, look out: there's usually some sort of personality shift.

Here's a typical scenario that might ring a bell for you. You're at another one of those rubber chicken, what-the-hell-are-those-vegetables, dinner meetings, seated at a table with five or six people you've never met before, when it suddenly occurs to you that you're not comfortable. The truth is, you're not exactly thrilled to be there (but you need to be); instead, you have a deep longing for something familiar, like your sofa and the remote control.

Introductions are made around the table, but you immediately forget the names — unless a name belongs to someone you might want to do business with. You then exchange pleasantries and talk about your line of work, but no one is really very interested — that is, unless *you* are someone *they* are hoping to do business with. There's a definite wall between you and your real self as you keep the conversation flowing. You know it's there, that wall, but you don't know what to do about it. Building it has become a habit. It's because you're all tied up in saying the right thing; and in the process, you've become an entirely different person.

It sounds like I'm saying we don't care about or aren't interested in the people we meet and work with, doesn't it? The irony is we do; we just don't behave like it. We're too busy making the almighty impression.

In our quest to impress, we rely heavily on our best keep-your-feet-off-the-furniture persona. And this is ever so prevalent at one of those aforementioned dinners, or business meetings, sales presentations, and various other work-type affairs. We overcompensate. We're pushing to be our best, but we're about as convincing as an anorexic at a smorgasbord. What's truly sad is we lose our magic exactly when we need it the most; and we forego our most unique and fascinating self when we lose our spontaneity, our authenticity.

It's not uncommon under such strained circumstances to act proper, stilted, reserved, formal, and ohhhh so very appropriate. We do things like break our dinner rolls far more carefully — we keep the crumbs on the plate with the precision of a log roller — use the butter knife FOR the butter, scoop our soup instead of slurping it, attempt to throw in bits of worthwhile conversational soundbites between big bites of food, and smile frequently (every moment's a Kodak moment).

What's more remarkable than anything else under the circumstances, though, is that we do one of two things: We act like our mother, or like our father. That is to say, when we're under pressure of any kind with other people, many of us take on the personality traits of one of our parents (by the way, we usually emulate the more dominant parent). This can occur no matter what the size of the audience, whether one or 1,000. It can happen at one of those banquet tables, a board meeting, sales call, new business pitch, or major speech.

The next time you feel ill at ease with people, notice *your* mannerisms, the tone and tempo or your voice, your facial expressions, the sounds you utter, your nervous tics, the way you move. Chances are that some or all of these will mimic the behavior of your mother or your father, or even an authority figure from your early years. (For me, it was Sister Carla, my fourth grade teacher.) The point is that when we're under pressure, most of us take on a personality that is not the best of who WE *really* are; in fact, it's not us at all! Think about it: Are you the same person at one of those banquet business deals as you are when you're in the kitchen talking to your best friend? Why not?

Here are some indications that you're not being yourself (and the people you're with are not being their true selves either): laughing a bit too loudly; using too many "uhs" and "ahs;" overly animated expressions (at statements that don't deserve them); sitting up painfully straight; small talk that seems to disintegrate into even smaller talk; continually wiping the corners of your mouth with the linen napkin; and giving a business card to the same person twice. These are all signs that you're not actualizing your own unique personality. Unfortunately, it's a vicious cycle that digs a deeper and deeper groove.

When you've wiped the last bit of Baked Alaska from the corner of your mouth, you drag this overdone, yet keenly polished persona (that doesn't really belong to you) to the speaker's podium. Some of the behaviors your audience might notice while you're up there include: rocking back and forth; tilting your head at an awkward angle; talking too slowly or too deliberately; too many "uhs" and "ahs"; stammering; sniffing; tugging repeatedly at the same piece of clothing; manically clearing your throat; constantly emphasizing the wrong words; flushed neck and cheeks; wringing the hands; and pupils that seem to enlarge at the slightest distraction. Once again, these symptoms simply don't occur in casual conversation in the kitchen with your best friend.

Why the difference? According to the "Miller" theory, when we enter the world of business, there's so much riding on our image, our identity, that we end up adopting a dual personality — our true self and our business self. (Incidentally, the higher up the success ladder we go, the greater this dichotomy can become.) So instead of making the type of impact we want to have on others — coming across as spontaneous, genuine, caring, personable, confident, and at ease — we communicate instead from a level of pretense. And pretense is like Saran Wrap: The other person can see right through it.

Pretense is not always an overt display either; it can be quite subtle. In fact, we often alienate others with our subtext — things that are unsaid, or things below the surface. Did you know that only about 7 percent of our message is transmitted through the words we choose? That means that approximately 93 percent of what we communicate is conveyed through body language, vocal quality, facial expression, etc. And fully 88 percent of our "message" passes directly into the subconscious minds of our listeners. So if we're not genuine, our audience will be onto us immediately. They want to connect with someone REAL; they're alienated by pretense and deception.

You see, it's the aforementioned cycle that keeps us from solidly connecting to our "audience" — to other human beings, the ones we need the most, who make our professional worlds go round. Without the human connection, there is no other connection. People want people, especially in the hi-tech times of the '90s. We crave the human touch. But we can only make a sincere connection to others when we allow ourselves to *be* — ourselves.

Being real is the first step toward becoming a more effective communicator and presenter, whether you're at one of those banquet tables or at the podium. If you're able to be your true self in front of an audience — as opposed to adopting some inauthentic business persona — you'll be more likely to say interesting things; appear confident; animate naturally and appropriately; have inflection in your voice; and deliver your speech with real zing. You might even be spontaneous — wow! — always a winning way to be. All in all, you'll have appeal. People will like you. That's the first step in making the human connection. And I believe when you truly connect with others, you can get anything you want from them.

So the next time you're "on," ask yourself who are you "doing," and is it getting you what you want?

The following exercises will help to ensure that you're presenting your *real* self when it's *real* important.

1. Every time you're in front of an audience, pretend that you're speaking to someone you're comfortable with. For instance, when I'm in front of a group, I sometimes pretend that I'm talking to my daughter Shannon. She thinks everything I do is wonderful, which gives me permission to be myself. I'm always conversational when I have that mind-set.

2. Try to get the other person (or persons) to be themselves. If you're at ease, they will be, too. Stick to conversational items that are interesting, and be personable. Be a little vulnerable. Be in the moment and go with the flow. Let your dialogue be spontaneous. Don't think so much; just respond to the conversation at hand.

3. Stand in front of a mirror and converse like you would in a business setting. Take note of your overall presence. Is it you? Are you as natural and as free as when talking with your best friend in the kitchen? Watching yourself is one of the best ways to learn about yourself. If you have the equipment, set up a camera and videotape yourself; then play it back. If you're only able to record yourself in audio, do that instead. Hearing yourself, and seeing yourself, will help you to determine whether or not you have presence. The eyes and ears don't lie!

4. Notice how you behave with the various people at your office. Identify the ones you're most at ease with. Work at keeping your own "magic," your own personality, even when you feel stressed in the presence of those who represent authority.

5. Begin to take note of the people in your work environment whom you particularly admire. If your admiration is genuine, they'll probably be the people who are well liked by others. Stand back and assess their behavioral styles. Chances are that the people you admire appear confident, relaxed, and most importantly, connectable.

6. If you do carry those personality traits belonging to a parent or authority figure, see if you can identify the traits. Ask yourself if they complement your "package" or detract from it. If it's the latter, create an awareness each time you emu-

late a gesture, phrase, or look. You'll soon shed unwanted baggage.

7. Notice how other people relate to when you're in your personal demeanor and when you're in your business demeanor. Other people's reactions are the strongest methods of persuasion for getting you to change. When people react positively to you because you're real, it's very hard to revert to the old way of distancing yourself by being formal and pretentious. People will mirror you; what you are getting back from them will tell you what you're putting out.

8. Despite what your parents told you, talk to strangers. That makes for great rehearsal time.

9. Don't take your job so seriously. If you're losing your *self*, find something else to do professionally.

10. Relax, lighten up, and enjoy yourself and others. If you do, your communications and presentations will be terrific!

"You're going to love Miller... he's witty, he's funny —
just an overall great speaker..."

Chapter 4

GETTING COMFORTABLE

SETTING THE STAGE

People who don't like to speak — audience size notwithstanding — feel that way because speaking in front of others makes them uncomfortable. If this doesn't describe you, then you can skip this chapter. If it does, read on. This one's for you!

Prior to the AIDS crisis, fear of public speaking was the number one phobia among businesspersons in the United States. And at least 80 percent of the people we train at ExecuProv complain of some type of discomfort when all eyes are on them, such as while making a speech or presentation, giving a report or sales pitch, or even while doing something as ordinary as introducing themselves. Based on the comments of my students, the common denominator in their discomfort seems to be a feeling of tremendous responsibility that comes when: there's one of you; a bunch of them (the audience); and you're the one who has to do the talking. It's scary.

Sure, there are those who love the limelight, who don't want to share the stage with anyone, but that's not very common in the business community. Quite the contrary. Unless you're in sales, the prospect of public speaking usually conjures up about the same degree of enthusiasm as doing your laundry: You don't wanna, but you gotta. In fact, when faced with the "chore" of speaking in front of others, many people report a sensation of feeling physically weighted down; they view the task as drudgery.

Others say that they feel frightened and panicky, even freaked out, when they know it's their time to speak. Now, "freaking out" can lead to a myriad of problems — everything from slightly quickened breathing to a full-blown panic disorder. However, the most common side effects are: shallow breathing, cotton mouth, shaky or weak limbs, nausea, heart palpitations, chattering teeth, tight jaw, numbness of the fingers and toes, quivering lips, tripping over the tongue, flushed skin, flaring nostrils, throat clearing — all of which can result in escalating levels of anxiety. Further, each speaking experience can produce a different combo platter of the above reactions, depending on an array of variables and an individual's response to them.

The degree of nervousness we experience while speaking in public will govern how much adrenaline pours into our system during the "ordeal." That adrenaline "rush," as it's called, is actually our friend if used properly, because the quick release of that hormonal substance gives us an immediate boost in energy level. And we need energy to perform, to get that "ummmph" behind the first words we speak, and to carry us through with power until the final words fall off our tongues.

Most people who experience "horrible physical sensations" try to squelch and subdue them, because these sensations are unpleasant and leave people feeling "not right." That mental calisthenic only makes matters worse, however. Remember, adrenaline is energy. If you block that energy, you'll blow yourself up, metaphorically speaking, by internalizing the rush. On the other hand, if you allow the energy to be released, your body will even itself out. Even better, you can make use of that sudden burst of energy in much the same way a booster is used when launching a rocket.

One way to manage the overwhelming supply of adrenaline is to breathe diaphragmatically. (We'll be covering the subject of proper breathing more fully in the next chapter, but for now, just recall the way you breathe during biofeedback, yoga, Lamaze, or simply when you feel relaxed.) What I'm referring to are slow, even, rhythmic breaths that emanate from the diaphragm — the muscle located right above your stomach. Proper breathing will abate the sensation of hyperventilation that many people experience right before or during speechmaking, and will help to diminish other physical complaints as well.

According to the "Miller" philosophy, if you *feel* good, you'll be much more likely to greet the prospect of public speaking with enthusiasm. But how can you enjoy yourself when you feel bad? It's like trying to enjoy an airplane meal mid-flight when the plane is upside down. Talk about out of control!

Now, you probably don't think about how you're feeling or how you're coming across when you're just chatting with friends; the words simply flow out of you. But when you're not feeling well physically (perhaps due to a cold, the flu, surgery, etc.) or when something is upsetting you emotionally, talking may be a real effort. The same thing happens with public speaking. The idea, then, is to get *comfortable*. But how?

Well, your discomfort stems from fear, and fear is a learned behavior. That means you can *unlearn* it. The more you speak, and enjoy it, in a feel-good state, the more you'll recondition your psyche to associate public speaking with positive experiences, both physical and mental. This will occur little by little, step by step, speech by speech.

Here are some suggestions for retraining your point of view (conscious or unconscious), and for various ways of getting physically comfortable:

1. Practice the diaphragmatic breathing techniques in the next chapter. After a time, they'll become unconscious responses to stress, and you'll feel more in control.

2. Practice visualization. Picture yourself in your most peaceful and pleasant surroundings just before it's your turn to "go up."

3. Pretend that you're not really you. (I do this all the time.) That is, when it's time for you to be "on," simply play a character. Leave your *self* behind and take on a different persona — one that's appropriate, of course! (For example, pretend you're someone who loves to speak, or imitate someone you admire.) Many actors do this to handle their stage fright when doing live theater. This will get you over the hump and on your way to being you (like you in the kitchen). (More on this in a later chapter.)

4. When you begin to feel uncomfortable, distract yourself. Get very mental: try to figure out a bridge hand, a chess move,

the square root of some number. Detaching your mind from the fearful things you're producing will help keep things in check.

5. Review your material in your head. Methodically recap the strategic points you want to make, no matter how long your talk is. For instance, it could be as short as, "Hi, my name is..." You can't believe how many people forget their names for a few seconds.

6. Talk to the person sitting next to you, if it's not an impolite time to be doing so. Get into their stuff; you'll forget about your own. Improv actors are trained to keep their focus on the other actors, not on themselves. This keeps them from being self-conscious and getting mentally paralyzed. They simply react to the other players.

7. Conjure up the image of your greatest hero, whether it's a movie star, one of history's greats, or someone in the office whom you admire.

8. Try a series of affirmations. "I'm not afraid of anything or anyone" is a good one. Since your subconscious doesn't know truth from fiction, it will imprint this statement on your deepest thoughts, and good things will follow. I currently have a student who has stickers everywhere that read "I don't need this job," which is what actors tell themselves prior to an audition in order to take the pressure off. It's simply a metaphor for "No big deal."

9. Recite some of your favorite, most powerful adages, quotes, or words of wisdom, whether they be from Mom ("...nothing to be afraid of...") or other great leaders. For a little comic relief, try Lily Tomlin's, "Don't forget, we're all in this alone," or on a more serious note, Winston Churchill's all-inspiring pearl, "The definition of power is the ability to go from failure to failure with enthusiasm." Whatever works for you, think it. Do it! My daughter once gave me a bumper sticker that read, "Don't take life so seriously; it's only a temporary situation." I think of that adage frequently when I'm anxious about something; it takes the edge off.

"I am projecting my voice. As you can see, it's all over the room!"

Chapter 5

Take a Deep Breath and Count To ... Yourself

Proper Breathing and Vocal Production

Did you ever open your mouth to speak and hear something faint, something distant, which resembles your voice — sort of? You were probably thinking: On what word will I fade out *altogether*? Or how about when your chest heaves up and out as you swallow large gulps of air — don't you feel like you might levitate or fly right out of there? Better yet, don't you wish you could? In this condition, you're like a vacuum cleaner gone amuck — gasping, sucking, blowing, sometimes sputtering, at all the wrong times and places.

Well, take a deep breath.

This may be one of the most important chapters in the "Miller" book. Why? Because it's about proper breathing, and breathing is at the core of all things when it comes to performing (which is very much akin to public speaking).

As mentioned in the previous chapter, many people dislike speaking in front of others because they feel physically uncomfortable while doing so. For most, the primary cause of this discomfort is a very simple one: their breathing is out of whack. You may already know that when you're anxious, you tend to breathe rapidly and unevenly. More importantly, your breathing will also tend to be shallow, which leads to hyperventilation. In that state, you're never going to have a good time, let alone be able to focus on saying something important or convincing.

27

Oddly enough, breathing properly has everything to do with not only your comfort level, but also the sound that you produce. I advise all of my students to first master the art of diaphragmatic breathing before moving on to anything else; because if they don't, there's no way they'll be physically comfortable or capable of producing a good sound later on, when they have to get up in front of people and speak.

For those of you who are singers, you know where your diaphragm is and how to use it. But if you've never studied vocal technique, don't worry; it's not hard to learn, and your diaphragm is easy to locate. In fact, it's the muscle just above your stomach that regulates your breathing. It's what kicks in and breathes automatically for you while you're asleep. You also use it when you laugh, cry, whisper, yell, and when you're completely relaxed. But when you're nervous, you tend to breathe shallowly, utilizing only the top half of your lungs. As a result, you don't feel well physically, and when you speak, your voice sounds shaky, strained and/or labored.

Meditation, yoga, biofeedback — all use diaphragmatic breathing as their starting point, their fundamental precept; and so should you. Your diaphragm is your friend. With proper use, it can calm you in times of anxiety. It also enables you to amplify your voice without the aid of a microphone. In addition, your diaphragm allows you to tap into a wide vocal range, so that you end up sounding interesting and, most importantly, professional. But how?

Well, I'm not a voice expert, but I do know that when air is pushed up through the esophagus and past your vocal nodes, you get quality and resonance, contrast and variety — a real vocal boost. And that vocal boost gives you power; there's something about a powerful voice that commands respect. Stage actors (and great speakers) use great vocal technique all the time. It's one of their secrets. In fact, that's largely what holds the attention of their audiences. Great vocal technique results from the way in which actors use their voices; they experiment, play, and maximize their natural vocal qualities.

If you're having trouble envisioning this whole diaphragm and sound thing, think about newborn babies and how loudly they cry. Recall, too, the different pitches and tones they're able to produce. Did you ever wonder why you can hear the cry of a baby even if you're at the opposite end of the house? It's because that tiny baby is breathing diaphragmatically, and projecting its voice like crazy!

Remember, you have only two things with which to communicate: your face and your voice. You want to make the most out of both of them.

But let's focus on the voice for now. Once you've conquered the art of proper breathing — which, incidentally, will become hypnotic to you; an automatic response when you're under pressure, if you do your exercises regularly — then you'll be able to master good vocal production.

Without getting into a lengthy explanation, vocal production is essentially sound, your sound. If proper breathing is the basis for your method of vocal production or expression, you'll get the most out of the particular assortment of sounds that are inherent to your voice. Your voice is like your audio fingerprint; it's different from everyone else's. What a shame, then, so few of us use all the unique impressions housed within it.

Regarding vocalization, my biggest complaint is that most business professionals start their day without any vocal warmup. They spend the first hour on the phones, or talking at a meeting or before a group (God forbid!), warming up at everyone else's expense. Think about an actor at a performance. No trained actor would take the stage, any stage, without first vocalizing backstage in order to get his or her voice sounding full, rich, and awake. We should all do the same. You can warm up anywhere — in the shower, in the car on the way to work, walking through the parking lot. There are loads of opportunities every morning, noon and night.

How to vocalize? Talk out loud. Speak up. Speak out. Talk at different volume levels. Speak from the very bottom of your voice to the very top. Laugh. Sing. Vent. You can even gargle! Experiment with variations in sound, pitch, cadence, pacing, and inflection. Do the vocal and breathing exercises at the end of this chapter. They're easy and tend to boost your energy level — another important "Miller" precept that will be covered a few chapters from now.

By the way, don't forget to work daily on building up your

diaphragm. It's a muscle, so the more you work it, the stronger it'll become, and the more it'll support your vocal production. In addition, if you do the diaphragm-strengthening exercises regularly, proper breathing will soon become your automatic response during times when you're under pressure and feeling anxious.

To recap: Breathe properly for comfort and control; vocalize to get the most out of your voice. One of the most important benefits of mastering good breathing and vocal production techniques is consistency in performance. You can distinguish the pros from the amateurs, because the professionals are always solid, always perform with finesse and polish, always sound great. They impress their audiences with a strong presence that fills the room; and they command attention. People look forward to repeat performances by the pros, because they know the performances will *always* be good.

The following exercises will help you to become more of a pro (and less of an amateur!). Remember to do them daily:

First, make certain you're standing up straight and tall, with shoulders back, chest out. Good posture. If you want, stand against a wall or solid surface. Press your shoulders and back against that surface, and now walk forward. This is the posture you should have for practicing the breathing and vocal exercises.

BREATHING EXERCISES:

1. Bend over from your waist and let your arms and head hang down (bend your knees slightly if your back is straining). Slowly, VERY slowly, begin to inhale with an "sssss" sound to a count of 20. (Don't worry if you can't get up to 20; keep practicing, and you will!) As you are inhaling, bring your body back to an upright position VERY slowly, until you are standing erect and cannot take in another breath. Keep your chest high, but DO NOT LIFT YOUR SHOULDERS OR CHEST TO INHALE!! Imagine your upper body is in a vise to help you keep it as still as possible. The objective here is to exercise your lower internal and external oblique muscles, and to expand your LOWER lung capacity.

Once you have completely inhaled, begin exhaling VERY SLOWLY, again to the count of 20 (or less) on a "shhhh" sound until you have expelled all of the air that you possibly can. Then simply drop your jaw, and with your tongue relaxed down against the back of your lower teeth, let the air rush in to expand your lungs. DO NOT LIFT YOUR CHEST OR SHOULDERS!

The purpose of this exercise is to re-educate your body to breathe properly, expand your lower lung capacity, and strengthen the muscles surrounding the lungs and diaphragm. Do this exercise at least 5 times before making any speech or presentation. It will relax you, as well as giving you more control and support for your speaking voice!

NOTE: You can also do this exercise in the car (without bending); try to feel yourself expanding through your back against the seat while you inhale.

2. Standing tall, with your body in alignment, chest high and shoulders down, place your left hand behind you in the center of your back (this forces the chest to open up).

Begin inhaling on "ssss" to a count of 20, moving your right arm in a clockwise motion from your side, across your chest in an arc until you reach it straight up into the air. You want to reach the top at the same time as you complete your inhalation. KEEP YOUR CHEST AND SHOULDERS AS STILL AS POSSIBLE.

Begin exhaling on "shhh" as you bring your arm around (still clockwise) and down until it is again resting at your side. Then open your mouth (relaxed jaw!), and with your tongue resting against your lower teeth, let the air rush in silently. REMEMBER TO KEEP YOUR SHOULDERS AND CHEST STILL!!

Repeat these steps with the opposite arm.

The purpose of this exercise is to force the chest into open posture, and to practice pressing into your back (feel the resistance against your hand) while inhaling, in order to force the lower muscles to do the work for you, so that your throat is open and relaxed.

You can also do this exercise several times before speaking as a way of regulating your breathing, relaxing your body, improving your posture, and expanding your lung capacity, in order to give your speaking a real boost of energy!

3. Place your hand against your diaphragm and do any variation of "HAH! HAH! HAH! HAH! HAH! HAH!" Feel your diaphragm contract and release. You're building the muscle.

4. Take a diaphragmatic breath and begin talking, slowly releasing air from your diaphragm as you speak. Try to speak as long as possible before taking another breath.

VOCAL PRODUCTION:

1. Keeping your posture erect, open your mouth widely as you say loudly and deeply, "YAW, YAW, YAW, YAW, YAW, YAAAAAAAAAAAW." Drop your jaw as low as possible on the last "YAW." Project your voice, or as we say in the theater, throw your voice. In other words, speak big FROM YOUR DIAPHRAGM (don't yell) as you recite your "YAWs." Feel your diaphragm move.

2. Choose between trilling your "R's" and making a motor boat noise with your lips. Make either noise while turning your head slowly from side to side. Do this for a few minutes or so. It should warm up your throat.

3. Count from 1 (using your lowest voice) to 20 or more (using your highest voice) to stretch your vocal range. This is comparable to singing musical scales, which you can also do (in fact, singing of any type is a great warm-up). After you're able to reach 20, try to go beyond that number. You should be able to do that after a time.

4. Recite a poem, the Declaration of Independence, a famous speech, song lyrics — just talk out loud from a memorized piece. Speak up and say it with verve.

5. Pick up a magazine or newspaper and begin reading it aloud. Read it loudly, quietly, normally. Play around with your voice. Be spontaneous. Read in low tones, high pitches. Pick a page and read it in its entirety, even if it's an ad out of *Time* magazine. Be free and experimental. Focus on your voice. The more you practice, the more malleable your voice will

become, and the more interesting you will become.

6. Give your upcoming speech or presentation in front of the mirror. Talk from the diaphragm and use lots of vocal range. Experiment with different passages as you go about delivering your material. Try delivering each paragraph, each idea, in several different ways.

7. Make sure you warm up every morning and before *every* "performance" you give. The pros do it, and so should you.

8. Take a Halls or Ricola cough drop to clear your throat and nasal passages. They feel refreshing, and open your throat.

9. Don't drink anything too hot or too cold before you speak; drink only tepid fluids. Also, avoid drinking dairy products before speaking; they will create excess mucus in your throat.

*"Ohay pee-er-pia-a-pec-a pic-ul-everfs.
I'd much rather write with this!"*

Chapter 6

SAY WHAT?

Horizontal Mouth and Other Diction Afflictions

"Hi-um-namz-Jaw-Smee-an-um-gla-be-er-speak-N-hugh-day." What? What'd you say? The distorted faces, the displeased murmurs — they play back at you from across the room like a bad dream on reverb. Oh, great! Great way to have the audience react to the first words out of your mouth as you get up and introduce yourself.

I have my pet peeves when it comes to speaker deficiencies, and poor diction tops the list. It's the worst. I don't think there's any excuse for it. What the person above was *supposed* to be saying was, "Hi, my name is Jim Smith, and I'm glad to be here speaking to you today."

If part of your job is speaking to the public, whether it's a single person or a group of people, it's incumbent upon you to sound professional. In order to do that, you must pronounce your words clearly and cleanly. Unfortunately, speaking well is not something that our American culture trains us to do.

I've tried to trace the origin of speech patterns in this country as compared to the more eloquent patterns found in some European countries (that's my perception, at least), and have arrived at a theory — albeit somewhat fanciful — to explain the discrepancy. Here goes! Our forefathers were basically 86'd from their homefront and forced to come to America. A few years later, the colonists got their revenge: They dumped not only the

Queen and her husband, the mad King George, but also the speech patterns of their homeland. No more long, round sounds. No elocution lessons. No finishing schools. No finishing each word. Just 200 years of telling it like it is.

And while these rebels passed down a legacy and a highly publicized inalienable right — the First Amendment — no one ever mentioned that the first group of guys who wrote it into law weren't referring solely to content: They meant slur it when you say it, freedom of speech means freedom of speech, what the hell — who cares! As a result, we inherited a very American condition that I call "horizontal mouth."

See, in this country we talk mostly with our lower lip and jaw. Rarely do we use our upper jaw when we talk, so it remains fairly still. In addition, the majority of us don't open our mouths fully when we speak. We don't move our mouths around our words, so we can't phonate — can't get the sound out. Unfortunately, this means that a good percentage of business people suffer from at least a hint of the Valley Girl or surfer dude mouthal configuration.

In addition, although some words are easy to say, others require effort if we're going to pronounce them correctly; but we're not taught good diction like we are good manners. Most of the problem stems from our laziness when it comes to finishing each word as we say it. We tend to drop off the last letter or two. (This is why, when we admonish our children to say "thank you," we should also insist that they pronounce the "k" and the "u.")

So, as I've already pointed out, the diction of most Americans cannot be considered a source of national pride. In fact, on the whole, if we Americans lined up our mouths for an international verbal Olympics, there'd be no gold medals for this country!

This is unfortunate, because I believe that our diction is what either turns people on or off about us during first encounters. Listening to someone with poor diction grates against our audio sensitivities after a very short period of time. Sometimes our response is even unconscious: We don't know why we can't stand to listen to someone, but poor diction is often the overwhelming reason. Conversely, those who speak well — who pronounce their every word — seem to capture our ear. Interestingly, they are usually the people we instantly trust, too. Respect is a factor as well. I don't care how successful you are, how well dressed, how good-looking, how intelligent, how savvy — if you speak poorly, you lose points. On the other hand, when you enunciate, you have the opportunity to bolster your image and subtly communicate your professionalism.

This is where actors have the edge. They are made to study vocalization; they are trained to speak with precision. Vocal precision is first and foremost; it's as basic to performing as catching a ball is to football. If you haven't had the coaching, don't despair; there's still hope. With enough practice, good diction can become as automatic as slipping on your shoes, signing a check, or brushing your teeth. You won't think consciously about it; you'll just do it.

Diligent practice and repetitive good habits — aimed at conditioning your mouth, tongue and jaws to MOVE — will afford you the ease to communicate with a sound that's pleasing, respected, and worth paying attention to. When you combine good diction with proper breathing and excellent vocal production, you'll have all the essentials for a full pro delivery (we'll talk about style later). Think of these basics the same way you would the cement slab on which your house is built: It's the foundation.

One of the first things I tell my students is that a good actor is a good observer, so remember to notice other people's techniques as you go about doing your ExecuProv work. Soon you'll become aware of things you never noticed in people before. You'll begin to critique those who get up to speak, and you'll grade their presentations based on more than just content. You'll be able to identify why you liked or disliked individual presentations. Next, you'll begin to listen — really listen. You'll easily distinguish between those who have good diction and those who don't, those who have natural power and those who don't. Subsequently, you'll begin to listen and evaluate yourself, too.

One great homework assignment is to listen to your favorite singers. Barbra Streisand provides an excellent example of perfect diction. In her music, or even when she talks, she never misses a letter; she pronounces *everything*. Maureen McGovern, Linda Ronstadt, Mel Torme, members of the Manhattan Transfer — they're just a few who have what I call impeccable diction. That's why they're all so highly respected in their field; it's not just their musical abilities.

Listen to actors like Glenn Close, Meryl Streep, Jeremy Irons, Anthony Hopkins — there are so many. Make a list of your favorites, whether they're actors, newscasters, your business associates, friends. Who's good, and who's not? Learn from them. An attorney friend once told me that as a young artist, Maureen McGovern did not study professionally. Instead, she listened ardently to her favorite vocalist for hours each day: She learned to execute her lyrics perfectly by obsessively studying the works of Streisand.

Ask yourself, right now: Do I speak well? Do I sound professional? Do I have the personal sophistication needed for my position? If you're not sure how you sound, tape your voice. Play it back. What do you hear? Do you like it? Could you sound better?

We all can! Once again, I believe that anyone who talks to people needs good basic stage skills — good diction, of course, being one of them. In fact, many of those who already consider themselves good speakers and presenters could clean up their diction, too.

The following are your homework assignments for improving your diction (no matter how good you may think it is!). Even those of us who perform on a regular basis make diction exercises part of our daily workout regimen. After a time, you won't have to think about diction at all, because you will have consciously retrained what was previously your unconscious manner of speaking. Then you'll be able to focus on other important matters, like the message you're trying to get across.

Do these:

1. This is my favorite (my first drama coach made me do this when I was a small child): Take a pencil, not a pen, preferably one without a shiny finish on it, and place it between your upper and lower incisors (the teeth at the very front of your mouth). Now, speak slowly, OVER-pronouncing every consonant, every vowel — every letter as you talk out loud. Overdo your "T's", "D's", "R's", "S's" — really push your tongue against the edge of the pencil. Do it slowly. Take

your time. Do this for only about a minute the first few times, because your jaws may get sore, which is okay because you're building your jaw muscles (or as they say in the music business, "busting your chops"). Later on, you should be able to do the pencil exercise for up to five minutes a day. After 21 days of diligent practice, your diction should improve without your being conscious of it. After speaking with the pencil each time, remove it, but continue talking. You will notice that your mouth moves more easily, and that the sound is cleaner and clearer. You'll find that listening to your own voice has become a much more pleasant experience than in the past.

2. Tongue twisters are always great practice for improving diction. Try the following examples every day. Say them in the car. Say them fast. Say them from your diaphragm. Say them over and over. Really move your mouth around your words.

For the front of your mouth (this is great for warm up):
- Rubber baby buggy bumpers
- Toy boat
- Peter Piper picked a peck of pickled peppers
- Petra's pouch pinched Paula

To condition your tongue and get it moving:
- Red leather, yellow leather
- She sells sea shells by the seashore
- Lilly looks lightheaded laughing

For the back of your throat:
- Unique New York
- Hey, hi!
- Humdinger, Huckle Hank

Now, make a list of *your* favorite tongue twisters. Switch around from day to day.

3. Say "a-e-i-o-u" loudly and slowly. This will help promote proper breathing, as well as help with your diction. Each vowel should be over-exaggerated in order to really move your facial muscles. Again, a clear sound will emerge.

4. Do your "YAW-YAW" exercise for enhanced vocal production and diction.

5. Stretch your lips and tongue by moving them all about rapidly.

6. Do the trilling your "R's" or the motor boat exercise to get your diction muscles toned and ready to go.

7. Start listening to those around you. Are they pronouncing each and every word? Are they pleasant to listen to? Do they sound professional? Now, how about you? Do you sound professional? Really work at your diction. It will kick in when you need it the most, without your having to think about it.

8. After working on the above, read poetry out loud, pronouncing every solitary letter of every single, solitary word. If poetry isn't your thing, read the stock report, a menu, a contract.

9. Read stories to your children or grandchildren.

10. Sing the "Star-Spangled Banner" with soul.

11. Now, try some ideas of your own. The point is to work on your diction religiously. Condition those facial muscles that operate your mouth. Don't slack off for a day or two, or you'll slide back into that mush-mouth thing. Make diction workouts part of your everyday routine.

Chapter 7

WHAT WAS THAT?

Aware or Not Aware:
That Is a Problem

Great improv players must be able to instantly take in what's given to them by the audience and act on those suggestions. The scene will fail if they're not able to take in, assess, and absorb a number of particulars quickly. So, after learning the basic stage skills, students of improv begin to study ways of increasing their awareness levels — to notice more of what's going on in their immediate environment and with the people around them. As a result, they begin to take things in on a multi-faceted level, so to speak; they become more cognizant as they check things out more thoroughly, more perceptively.

Increased awareness leads to the ability to respond more quickly and appropriately to another person or to groups of people. It also fosters the capability for taking in, perceiving, processing, and feeding back to others more fully. Unfortunately, while this heightened awareness is a staple of the improv player's repertoire, it's not exactly the norm for the average person in the business community.

In order to become more alert, attentive, tuned in, and perceptive, we have to do things every day to enhance the strength of our mental muscles. This requires work, because most of us aren't inherently skilled at achieving total awareness. So if we want to have greater awareness of what's going on around us, we'll need to practice repeatedly, just like we do with the basic stage skills. Eventually, this way of observing will become as automatic as, well, clean diction.

The two most common obstacles to total awareness are pressure and preoccupation. I know they are for me. If I'm worried or stressed out about making the impression, the sale, the deal, or maybe even by how my hair is looking that day, I'm somewhat oblivious to the "who" and "what" of my environment. Or maybe I'm spacing out on something I need to finish, or have jumped ahead mentally to my schedule for the next day; so that while my body is there, my mind certainly isn't.

We're also robbed of awareness when our everyday situations become too familiar. If we live our lives with too much sameness, eventually things just become a blur; they don't attract our attention any more; they become practically non-existent.

I'm constantly observing business professionals in their everyday settings, and I can't tell you how many times I've known that these people don't have the slightest idea of what's going on around them or even where they are. If I were to ask them to close their eyes and take a quiz about what they'd just seen or heard, they'd most likely flunk. It's even happened to me.

Here's one for you: I was talking to a guy during one of those cocktail moments preceding a banquet that I didn't really want to attend anyway. I'd been chatting with him for several minutes when someone else walked up and joined us. (The face was familiar; we'd definitely met before.) I attempted to introduce them to one another, but didn't have the slightest idea what either of their names were. On that particular evening, I'd have paid a hundred bucks per name tag. It was especially embarrassing for me; after all, I teach the stuff!

The point is, many people — including myself, sometimes — aren't really "there" in the moment; they just pretend to be. (Ultimately, this leads to other problems, like listening disorders, which will be discussed in a later chapter.) The immediate problem for you, though, is that if you're not paying attention to the preliminary stuff, you won't be able to respond spontaneously and appropriately to the needs of those you come in contact with — especially the beneath-the-surface needs, the kind that leave the other person feeling understood and connected to you.

Good communication, then — whether it's with one or 100 — begins with attentiveness, with observation, with sensitivity. It starts here: you begin to notice everything around you. More specifically, instead of being so into you, you become more into "them" and "that."

Take a cue from improv players, who don't have the luxury of being "self" centered. Their job is to work as a team with the other players in the "scene," and to pay particular attention to the needs, whims, and points of view of the others. They must be quick; they must be able to respond instantly. Their trick is to completely let go of "self" — allow "self" to go with the flow, and watch and listen for every change and turn in the "scene." They must be aware of individual players' mood swings and dialogue shifts, and be prepared to go with them. They must play off even the most subtle fluctuations. This takes diligence. It takes practice. It takes a watchful eye, both literally and figuratively.

It may take time, but you, too, can increase your awareness level. How? First, by slowing down and doing what we call "being in the moment" — not thinking ahead, not hashing over what went before; clearing your head and just staying with every moment as it unfolds. That is the first rule, because then and only then can you begin to take in more of what's around you.

For example, check out the features on someone's face; take in what they're wearing, their vocal cadence. Do they have a particular smell from a cologne or perfume? What kind of watch are they wearing? What color are their eyes? Okay, now go beyond the superficial and get to the subtext, or what is unsaid, the messages beneath the surface. What kind of mood are they in? How are they really feeling? You can figure these things out if you observe such things as vocal tone and cadence, facial animation, body language, etc.

Study people individually. Pay attention to things you've never noticed before, like the way they move, walk, laugh. Critique the way they present themselves. Try to notice something new every time you come in contact with the people you interact with on a regular basis. I'm not referring to only those on the job, either. Try this at home.

Once you become more aware, you'll have a better chance of making that "human connection" we talked about earlier. People know when you're truly interested in them as opposed to when you're feigning interest. If you're genuinely observant, people pick up on your interest, and it makes them feel important. They're more apt to like and to trust you. And since we've previously agreed that we're all selling something, you're more likely to make the "sale" or the connection; and connecting and getting the other person to trust you are essential.

How many times have you walked into a "mixer" or meeting and actually caught the names of everyone you met? How easy is it for you to remember those names? How about the things people said to *you*: Can you recall specific things from their dialogues, or recount even the essence of the overall conversations? How many times were you thinking about something else as they were talking to you? Or looking around the room — scattered, distracted, *unaware*!

Now, ask yourself this: How many times has your inattentiveness or lack of awareness caused a problem for you?

Take heart! You can build your awareness just like a muscle — a mental muscle. Make sure you practice, practice, practice. The following exercises, done regularly, should make a significant difference in your awareness levels.

1. Sit quietly and let your mind go to whatever grabs your attention: the sound of traffic, the dishwasher running, a chirping bird. Just listen for a moment. Take your time. What do you hear that you hadn't noticed before? Then, gradually begin to take in other sounds around you. Study them. Now, begin to observe your surroundings visually. What do you see? Really look at what's around you. If it's the toaster on the counter, see if you can notice something different about that toaster. Walk into a room and try to notice something that you've never really noticed before. Now, expand this concept to include what you see and hear with regard to the people you encounter each day. You don't have to start out with everyone; you can take just one person at a time.

2. Next time you have a telephone conversation or go to a meeting, make sure you listen for names and content of the

message. Watch for body language when you can; really check things out. Forget about you!

3. Close your eyes and see if you can describe every detail on the face of your watch. Does it have a second hand? Most people are astounded when they try this. Think about it: it's something you look at all day long. Go on to bigger things like the dashboard of your car. Try something else that you see quite frequently. How about the lines around your eyes or brow? How many and where? Surprise, surprise, surprise!

4. Talk for a minute to the first person you come in contact with that day. Then, turn away or close your eyes and see if you can recount what the person was wearing. Get detailed: think about shoes, jewelry, what side their hair was parted on, lipstick color, the color and shape of a necktie. Write down these details, if you want; writing down what you observe is always a good way to lock things in. The idea here is to really zoom in on who and what is around you, and to then quiz yourself. This simple routine, performed regularly, will increase your awareness level, enabling you to "take in" with little effort as you go along.

5. Since we're all so into ourselves, see if you can find something new and different about you — your facial features, a nervous tic, a mole, a wrinkle. You'll be surprised! Truth is, we change every day, too.

6. Next time you're with a group of people at a party or a meeting, stay "in the moment." It will help you remember names, ideas, and important details. In particular, make it your job to remember names, always.

7. Devise some observation rituals of your own and do them regularly. Remember what I always tell my students: A good actor is a good observer. Make sure that's *your* starting point, so that you can improve your communication and presentation skills.

8. Bottom line: Check *it* out!

*"Okay, Mr. Rodin, I'm deep in concentration
and ready to be sculpted now!!"*

Chapter 8

PSYCHED AND CENTERED

The Fine Art of Concentration

First, let me point out the difference between awareness and concentration, because I don't want you to confuse the previous chapter and this one. Webster defines awareness as "having or showing realization, perception or knowledge." Concentration, on the other hand, is defined as the ability to "bring or direct toward a common center or objective; to focus." In short, awareness is being conscious of something; concentration is the ability to focus on it.

In improv terms, according to the "Miller" credo, concentration is the ability to stay where you are in thought, idea and reaction, fully and completely, until the next sequential moment transpires. In other words, you're *not*: in and out of your thoughts; scattered; unable to grab hold mentally and work the thought; or unfocused as to where you are, who you're with, why you're there, what you're doing, when it is — at any time.

The ability to concentrate is a real art.

In my opinion, it's also one of the hardest fundamentals to master. We face a constant barrage of both internal and external stimuli, which makes mental interference very common, even normal. In addition, when we feel threatened by any form of adversity, be it physical or mental — and for most of us it's usually mental — we often choke, clutch, and freeze. Our eyes get big, our faces get still; we're disconnected. It's not exactly an out-of-body experience; instead, we're literally out of our minds. Thoughts that we had a firm grip on suddenly slip away like muddy pigs.

Lack of concentration in the face of physical adversity makes sense: we need to be able to survive. It seems like mental stress should be easier to handle, but for some people it's not. I tell my acting students that they must develop a "thick" concentration level in order to stay focused, in order to stay on track with their message even if the roof falls in. Most business professionals, however, have what I term a "thin" concentration level, which means they're constantly falling prey to that villain, distraction.

Hey, we're all pulled off track sometimes when we speak in front of others, but some people have a devil of a time remembering what the hell they were talking about. The result: sheer horror. This is humiliating, and also indicates a lack of professionalism. The effects compound themselves, too — in the extreme, one could suffer a massive nervous breakdown right there at the foot of the lectern. So lapses in concentration can be a death sentence for the presenter/communicator.

Once you learn to concentrate deeply, however, mental stress can be handled consistently and effortlessly. You'll be able to re-access a thought that drifts before a split second splits by. Sure, you may get distracted, but you'll get pulled back quickly by your center, because you're deep into it. You'll regain your composure (the truth is, people won't even know you'd lost it). You won't be fazed, frazzled, or ruffled under any circumstances. You'll be unflappable, conditioned, trained.

Here's an extreme example of how training and conditioning can improve your ability to handle adversity. I once had a student who was so thoroughly schooled in the art of concentration that during a major earthquake, he continued with his ad campaign presentation while the rest of the people in the room were diving under the conference table. Without skipping a beat, my student, Paul, had the presence of mind to grab his art boards and join the others beneath the table. Cramped but determined, he continued his train of thought and his sales pitch; and when the shaking stopped, everyone laughed like hell. (Incidentally, Paul got the account; the client liked his spontaneity and ability to concentrate!)

As another example of what training can do for you — this one from my own files — I once did a summer play, a scripted work, in an outdoor theater. Without warning, rain began pouring down on us during a performance. Improv- trained as I was, I instantly created a line about why the character playing opposite me hadn't gotten his roof repaired yet. The audience burst into applause. I held for it, and then kept right on going.

The need to be able to concentrate easily and naturally is a "must have" for improv players, but they never force such focus. They come by it easily, because they've been able to tune out all distractions and stay in the moment, stay in the process, to go deep within and be anchored by the center of their purpose.

What I want you to think about is finding that anchor point, the place within you that feels secure, stable, rock- steady. There's no magic or mystery about getting there: You simply have to tap into that core and lock yourself in. It's like buckling the seatbelt in your car; it keeps you from sliding and bumping all around when the unexpected happens. Similarly, you need to strap your mind to your concentration core to keep your mind from scooting about. Once you've done that, you can let that core guide you as you travel verbally through any speech, presentation, or strained communication (for instance, a confrontation).

Remember the importance of all the things we've talked about so far. Proper breathing keeps you comfortable. Good diction makes you worthy of attention. Awareness helps you attend to the "who," "why," "where," and "what" of your environment. With concentration, you now have focus, which enables you to take in, and stay with, the matters at hand. By mastering these skills — breathing, diction, awareness, and concentration — and then integrating them into your daily life, every communication experience will become easier and more pleasurable for you.

The following exercises are intended to work your concentration muscle, and are the same ones I prescribe for my acting students. If you do these exercises regularly, you'll develop the "thick" concentration level that I alluded to earlier. And while I can't guarantee that you'll make it through an earthquake with the same aplomb as my student, Paul, I can assure you that the more "normal" distractions you're likely to encounter while giving a speech or presentation will no longer throw you!

1. First, clear your mind of all thoughts. Literally shake your head as a symbol of doing just that.

2. Stand in front of the mirror and hold your hands up and open, with your palms facing the mirror. Now, move your hands as slowly as you can, focusing on your hands as you see them in the mirror. GO SLOWLY. **The more slowly you go, the deeper your level of concentration.** Ideally, this exercise is done with a partner rather than alone. Here's how: Face each other, palms matching and nearly touching. You take turns leading the activity, while precisely mirroring every movement of the hands. After doing it for a while, you will feel a sense of stillness, a calm, quiet feeling that lets you know you're anchored. That's a feeling I want you to become very familiar with, very accustomed to.

The following is called "space work," and it's the best training I know of for training your concentration muscle. Space work is fun, and quite a challenge, too:

3. Do any activity like you normally would: Make a salad, brush your teeth, thread a needle, comb your hair, ready the dirty dishes for the dishwasher, swing a golf club. Now, do this activity again without the benefit of having the objects to work with. In other words, you'll pretend to have the objects in your hands; they're just invisible. Next, do the activity, without the objects, in slow motion, as slowly as you possibly can. (Remember, the slower you go, the deeper your concentration level.) Be consistently slow; don't get erratic by speeding up, slowing down,, going even slower, speeding up again, etc. The trick is staying even and consistent. This is actually very difficult to do, but when you achieve it, that's when you'll know that you're mastering concentration. The more consistently and smoothly you're able to do the activity, the more you've mastered your ability to focus. Do this activity for at least 3-5 minutes. If you're dealing with opening or closing a cupboard door, picking

something up from a countertop, loading the dishwasher, etc., are you being consistent with the height, location, and placement of things? That requires a great deal of concentration.

4. A fun variation of the above exercise is to stand in front of a mirror, close enough to see your facial features. Now, animate your face in slow motion. Pretend you've just had cold water thrown in your face, you've been slapped, you're about to sneeze — pick something you can have fun with. Now, do it in slow motion.

5. Read a paragraph of dialogue from a magazine or book; then quickly put it down and try to paraphrase what was said. The more quickly you can read and then re-tell, the sharper your concentration.

6. Here's a variation on the old "Concentration" television show. Take a normal deck of cards, spread them out face down on a table, and try to match them up as quickly as you can. You'll need to focus each time you turn a card over so that you can remember its placement. Silly, maybe, but it does build and thicken that concentration level of yours!

7. Stare at an object for a while. Really notice everything about it. Now, turn your back and write a detailed description or draw it. When you intently study such an object — be it a key chain, a television set, a computer keyboard, etc. — just focusing completely on that object, you'll tune out any other thoughts and feel "locked in." Now, try to discover something new about it. That's the feeling you want to begin to foster, so that when you're learning a speech, going over your notes for a presentation, or addressing a group, you can stay on each detail IN THE MOMENT — RIGHT THEN, RIGHT THERE.

8. Take a certain portion of your speech or presentation and begin to memorize it. Stay with each sentence until you know it verbatim. Tedious exercise, I know, but it's a great workout for focus.

9. Listen to the lyrics of one of your favorite songs. Try to duplicate the way it's sung. As you sing along, really stay with

each word you're singing at the moment; don't jump ahead. Really enjoy what you're singing AS you sing it.

10. There are probably other concentration exercises you can make up on your own. The guidelines for developing them are that whatever you're doing, you get the sense of getting lost in it, that feeling of stillness, of complete absorption, of totally detaching from everything around you while you're engaged in the process.

Concentration exercises do two other things for you. One, they automatically assist you in your ability to be spontaneous; and spontaneity (Chapter 13) is the heart of the "Miller" training program and the root of all improv. And number two, concentration exercises add mass to your memory muscle. It makes sense that if you're really into something at the time it's taking place, you'll be more likely to remember it; and if you commit it to memory, chances are you'll be able to recall it at a later time. Those who can recall get "A's." Think on that for a while!

"I'm looking at you and you're looking at me,
so that means we're together."

Chapter 9

THE EYES HAVE IT

And They Need to Make Contact

I won't belabor the issue of eye contact, although I do want you to realize how powerful and important good eye contact can be. Think about it: Short of actually touching someone, the connection of one pair of eyes to another is the only means we have for physically connecting with others.

It's been said the eyes are the mirror of the soul. That's entirely possible. One thing for certain, though, our eyes are our most revealing feature in terms of transmitting what kind of mood we're in, where we're coming from, and whether we're open and available or not. It's through the eyes that we first meet; and I don't mean on just a "How do you do" basis. I'm talking about meeting on a much more personal level, where we either connect or don't connect. And that first encounter is an all-important one, because it can decide the course of the relationship, whether personal or professional. It's during that initial moment of eye contact that we often decide whether we like or dislike someone.

Forget about psychology for a minute, though, and let's look at eye contact in terms of what it means to improv actors. After all, what the actors learn and the materials they have to work with are the crux of what I'm teaching you; and eye contact is one of the first things they study in improv training.

Eye contact is important to improv players for a number of

reasons. First, it's impossible to fully "respond and react" to the other players without looking them right in the eye. Responding and reacting are all the actors do when interacting in improv scenes. Good eye contact helps to establish stage rapport.

Let me put it another way: If you can't "read" the other actors, so to speak, you can't play off of them. If you can't play off of them in the split second timing required in improv comedy, the scene may meander, lack focus, or simply crash at the outset. In addition, when doing improv, you may have very few guidelines — often unrelated particulars supplied by the audience — as to your starting point. By looking at, and connecting with, the eyes of the other actors, you get an instant feel for the relational status of the characters; and it's only then, as improv players learn, that the scene can actually begin.

The scene can be launched from a specific vantage point only because the actors connected, and then reacted and responded according to that initial connection. If you've ever watched improv comedy sketches, you may have noticed that while many scenes have no dialogue whatsoever, there seems to be a lot going on between the players. Simply put: They are communicating — responding and reacting — through the language of their eyes.

Well, much the same holds true for the rest of us when we're in one of *our* everyday scenes — be it a meeting, major speech, sales pitch, etc. We react according to that initial, or possibly ongoing, eye contact experience. For example, when we begin to connect with those in our audience (be it large or small), we truly get a sense of how to adjust our dialogue, approach, or attitude based on what we see in the eyes of others. We're able to do this if we're completely alert and tuned in to picking up those "eye messages."

We've already talked about the importance of making the human connection. Well, the starting point of that connection is good eye contact. It's through eye contact that we establish the initial, and hopefully long-term, memory connection with others. Think of it this way: What you see is what you get. The eyes of others often tell all; and so do ours.

Granted, different people will respond differently with regard to eye contact. For example, let's say you're speaking to a fairly large group. There will be many pairs of eyes, some of which seem eager and open to your message, while others appear distant and aloof. It's this second group, whose eyes seem the most removed from what you're saying, that will require the greatest eye penetration on your part. If you have the courage to stay with them — the other people's eyes, that is — you'll usually be able to break the barrier.

I always play to the "difficult" people (i.e., those who won't look at me, or who seem most detached in more than an optical sense) in the room first, so I can unify my environment. I don't want any one person to ruin the good and open vibes that I'm putting out; and I've learned from experience that one person's refusal to look me in the eye can sometimes demoralize me to the point that I become uncomfortable and self-conscious.

The hold-outs let's call them, can easily diminish the positive energy that initially greets a speaker. Let me tell you how and why. When you approach an audience and catch a pair of eyes that appear cold, hostile, disinterested, skeptical, or otherwise negative, your subconscious (if not your conscious mind) registers it in a nanosecond. If you're like most people, you react involuntarily to this information. In a heartbeat, you retreat or scan the room for another pair of eyes, looking for someone more receptive. The problem is, during that brief interlude, you've disconnected from your audience. And more often than not, you'll simply withdraw; instead of looking at your audience, you'll direct your focus to the floor, your notes, or even something on the wall. But without eye contact with the audience, there is separation. Separation divides and ultimately alienates.

There is hardly anything more powerful than a speaker or presenter who has the ability to attach himself or herself to others through strong eye contact. That's not to say that you should attempt to intimidate someone by staring them down or piercing them with your eyes. Instead, you want to be relaxed enough to make a smooth, easy connection. You want to say "hello" with your eyes, invite your audience in, so to speak, and then visit with them.

Remember what I said earlier about the principle of "respond and react," which is used to teach improv players how to attach and connect. Well, the same principle applies to each of us, even if we're not professional improv actors. You see, it's virtually impossible to accurately respond or completely react without a meeting of the eyes. So, as you go about your daily meetings, presentations, speeches, etc., try to assess the amount and degree of your eye contact. Is it always fleeting? Do you quickly look away? Are you comfortable looking at someone's eyes? Do you even notice whether or not you're making eye contact? If so, what are you getting out of it? What are you learning about the person on the other side of those eyes? Are you responding and reacting according to what those eyes tell you?

One last thing: The ability to make comfortable eye contact is a great way to seduce any audience. (And I don't mean this in a sexual context!). After all, we're no different than other performers — our job is to make our audiences fall for us. There's no better way to begin this process than through good eye contact. And as an added bonus, when we're making eye contact with others, we're focusing outside ourselves, which reduces our tendency to be self-conscious. It's one of the lessons we teach in improv class: Free yourself of inhibitions by focusing on the other actors.

The following are a few pointers and exercises to assist you in building your eye contact skills:

1. When you first meet someone, make sure you're looking into his or her eyes during the introduction. This is a great way to disarm someone and provide an opening for a true and genuine connection.

2. If you become intimidated while trying to maintain eye contact with someone, look at the bridge of the other person's nose. It'll appear to them that you're looking right into their eyes, even though you're not. This little trick gives you time to regroup and collect yourself (and deal with any feelings of self-consciousness).

3. The first time you make eye contact with an individual, maintain the eye contact for at least five seconds. This may feel like an eternity, but it allows sufficient time to make the connection. By doing so, you'll have provided enough time for a strong and solid connection, which will enable you to more easily reconnect with that person in the future.

4. Spend time talking to strangers (in safe places, of course), and make eye contact with them when you do so. This allows you to practice your eye contact drills without any risk.

5. Notice other people's eye contact patterns and their reactions to yours. Is it easy for them to keep eye contact with you? Are you relaxed and inviting with your eyes, or are you too intense? Take note of other people's reactions. There's a lot to be learned from this exercise.

6. Each time you make a presentation, try to make eye contact with every individual. Work the room, as they say, until you've "touched" everyone. If the audience is large, try playing to different individuals in groups. Break up the room into clusters and make eye contact with one person, then another, as your eyes go from group to group. By doing this, the audience gets the impression that you've connected with them, even though you may not have looked directly into each individual pair of eyes.

7. This last exercise is a mind blower! Look in the mirror and make eye contact with your own eyes. What do you see when you look into yourself??!!!!

"Where's that podium? Today's the big one. I'm up!"

Chapter 10

Up and At 'Em

Building Your Energy Level

Low energy. There's nothing more destructive to a great sales pitch than a low energy level. Without energy, you can't connect. If you can't connect, you can't "sell"; and as I said earlier, we're all selling something.

Although I don't know a lot about physics, I do understand that there's nothing more powerful than energy. Everything is transmitted by it — whether it's a bullet train or a fleeting thought. Think about it. I certainly have. In fact, there was a time when I compared the energy level of everyone around me to some "thing." For example, when my girlfriend droned on, I pictured a slow-motion vacuum cleaner. While an actor bitched and complained, I imagined my blender on puree. My hyperactive adolescent became a Piccolo Pete firecracker; and my overweight, couch potato neighbor became a cement mixer trying to shift out of first gear on a steep hill. Amazing!

Later, I began to study and evaluate the energy of speakers, salespeople, and others who tended to be — and needed to be — in charge of their situation. I discovered that the ones I liked best had a strong energy level. That didn't mean they were loud or overbearing. Rather, they had an intensity, a presence, that held my attention; there was something about them that I couldn't detach from. I've come to realize that "something" was personal energy. The people I was drawn to had put it out, emitted it, transmitted it; and I had received it.

Consider this: You've seen speakers or presenters who have center stage. Their material is good, even interesting, but for some reason you're bored to tears. Your mind goes to your to-do list: "Well, I need to wash the car, and then go to the cleaners. No, I'll finish that report first." When you return to the listening cycle, you hear the speaker saying things like, "Aaaaannnnddd, wwwwweeeeelll gggeeeeennnttttttlemeeee..." Your mind drifts away again.

A low energy level is the reason that the presenter is speaking so slowly (and also the reason that you can't stay focused on him). He has no intensity, no fire. If he were a telephone, he'd be a dial tone. If he were a car engine, he'd be a sputtering idle. His lack of energy is evident in his voice — a monotone. The volume is constant or next to nothing, barely audible. His face is devoid of expression. Only the mouth moves. You wonder if possibly he's dead, and someone forgot to tell him.

You, the listener, and he, the speaker, gamely struggle through the presentation. (Ironically, that struggle is wasted energy.) If you're sensitive, you feel sorry for him. If you're insensitive — or just hate to waste time —you become agitated. Whatever the reaction, you can be sure that what you *don't* feel is a HUMAN CONNECTION with this individual. Why, then, would you buy what he's trying to sell you?

Let me reiterate: We all need to realize that until we connect with others, we cannot effectively inform or persuade them of anything — no matter how good our message or product. And if we don't transmit energy to our audience, whether it's one or 100, we won't make that connection.

Consider, for a moment, stage performers and film actors: If they had no intensity, no verve, no energy in their performances, you wouldn't respond. Instead of reacting to them by experiencing emotions or feelings, you'd just hear words and see movement. However, good actors always prepare beforehand by stimulating their energy, so that by the time they begin the first line of the performance, their energy is available and can be used for punctuating their delivery.

Think about a stove. If you're a burner, you can be turned down for low impact or turned up high, depending on what's appropriate or the response that's desired. It doesn't matter at what level you're cooking, just so you're cooking! But first, you must make sure you're turned on!

Here's another analogy, what I call the "velcro theory": Assume your left hand has this prickly, sticky velcro stuff on it, and that it represents the nice, brisk, high energy level you feel when you begin to talk to your audience. Since your audience will always mirror you, pretend that they are your right hand, and that in mirroring you, they will have their prickly, sticky velcro receptors stimulated and ready the minute they see or feel yours. Put these two hands (i.e., you and the audience) together at the same level of intensity, and they will form a strong connection; that is, the velcro — or energy — sticks. Your energy stimulated the energy of the audience, or they were energized by the expectation of seeing you. Now you've got their attention; they're open to whatever message you intend to give. They're receptive, because you've successfully transmitted your energy. Without that initial release of energy, however, the audience won't respond.

If we look again at the "velcro theory," we notice that without your energy (left hand velcro), there's no way that the audience's energy (right hand velcro) can hook on to yours. Those two hands would simply slip off one another. The end result? No connection!

If that concept is difficult to grasp, here's another way to look at it. You know how it is when someone walks up to you and suddenly screams in your face. You may not immediately scream back, but a feeling wells up inside you — a surge, a release that almost feels chemical. Well, that's simply energy responding to energy.

Now, who knows how you'll handle that immediate "connective" energy, but it's there; it's real. Perhaps we're all part of that Jungian collective unconscious (whereby we're all supposedly attached to one another), and that's why we react so instantly to whatever energy is directed toward us, and mirror each other's energy fields. Once again, if we don't display any energy, no one can connect to us.

You can spot another example of the energy mirroring process when you see people greeting each other at the airport.

Notice that if one person begins to cry, the other reacts, usually with a similar response. (They may not cry, may not show it, but chances are they're feeling an energy that's specific and/or identical to the energy they're encountering.) And as a bystander, you too get pulled into that energy and begin to experience the emotions as well. Energy is contagious!

Here's another way to think of it: Picture one of those ornaments that you place on your coffee table at Christmas time — the one with the reindeer inside and all those snowflakes. Let's pretend that the snowflakes are your energy particles. When you shake the ornament, the particles go every which way; they're vibrant and active. But when those same flakes just sit at the bottom of the ornament, there's no activity. *No energy.* Like a *statue.* There's only stillness.

When we display zero energy, our "flakes" just stay at the bottom of us. We need to shake up our particles if we want them to mingle with someone else's. If we want to connect, we have to have output. Very simply, that means that we have to "put out" — energy, that is.

As I was struggling with the idea of energy and how to convey it to my students, I decided to consult the dictionary. *Webster's* defines energy as: "force of expression," "inherent power," "capacity for action." These meanings express my point beautifully — if you don't use your innate power, your unique force of expression, and your God-given capacity for action, you can't effectively put yourself or your point across.

An interesting sidenote is that *Webster's* also defines energy (as it relates to physics) as "the capacity for doing work." This further punctuates the point I wish to make. We're all doing work of some type; and underlining it with a state of "capacity" is essential.

Another thought is that energy perpetuates itself. I know of many an actor who, exhausted but having to perform anyway, pulls from the core of his or her energy base and achieves great work. In the process, the actor also manufactures additional energy. It's just like with physical exercise: the more energy you expend, the more energy you create.

We're all unique, so everyone's energy field and his or her display of it will be different. Most of us fall into one of two energy categories: *inverted*, which is a little softer, quieter, sub-dued, restrained, confined; and *exverted*, which is usually louder, more animated, more expressively diversified (noticeably so), and bold. Neither is right nor wrong. Some of us are a mixture of the two, or fall somewhere in between. In any event, all of us have a great deal of energy that we *don't* use, especially when we're making a speech or giving a presentation. When we're among people we don't know, or if we're feeling confronted, we tend to suppress our energy, to invert it. We withdraw, pull back, build a wall. When we do that, however, there is no way to make that much-needed connection. Once we release the energy, we provide the opportunity to get back what we put out. And to get what we really want — a response!

So don't ever forget how critical it is to convey energy during that important speech or sales call. Remember, your audience cannot resist your energy. Remember, too, to begin your speech or presentation with a release of energy. A big burst of it grabs attention. Without attention, no audience. No audience, no sale.

In fact, when you're on stage — and most of you do what we call "live" performances a good deal of the time in your work — you need to really put out, because there's something weird about how quickly energy dissipates. As actors doing live theater will tell you, they really have to "pump," really have to "put it out," because a certain amount of the energy they're projecting to an audience will automatically disappear, evaporate, or fall into that mysterious gap between the edge of the stage and the first row (not to mention the last row). For this reason, every actor will tell you that he or she always plays to the *back* row. Energy has to extend to cover the entire room. Maybe you haven't thought of it this way before, but we're all performers, and we need bursts of energy in order to come across to our audience.

When we talk about expending energy to attract and hold the attention of others, or to make a point, we're not talking about screaming, or coming on too strong, or being imposing or overbearing. We're simply suggesting that you come *alive* and use your natural resource, energy, as the foundation for being a great speaker and/or presenter. Actors do it. Why shouldn't you?

And another thing: Great actors are only great because they're consistent. A good deal of this consistency comes from a free-flowing, automatic energy field. You've probably heard the term "cold readings" — that's when actors go in for auditions, pick up the script, and have to get right into the part *on the spot*, without any prior preparation. In other words, the actors have never seen the words they're about to deliver. In order to "sell" themselves during the audition, they'll need to come from a strong and authentic energy base. It's what makes the actors seem professional.

I, and a number of other directors I know, have cast many an actor because his or her intent with the characterization was so strong. The basis for that "sell" came from sheer energy (not the panty hose). We couldn't ignore it. We clearly reacted — and in a very positive way, too — to the actor's base of energy.

Ask yourself: How do *you* project your energy? To whom and where? Do you repress your energy out of fear? Are you actually sitting on your "self"? Do you respond to other people's energy, either positively or negatively? When you receive energy, do you transmit it back? Are you familiar with your different levels and degrees of energy? Do you ever experiment with them?

Begin to study the energy around you, whether it's with *things* or *people*. Get in touch with what stimulates your energy, and also begin to notice what shuts it down. A great actor is also a practiced observer. The more you take in about what's around you, the more you'll give out as a performer.

As I mentioned previously, what you'll want to achieve with regard to your energy output is consistency. You want to be able to count on yourself to pull up whatever energy is required for whatever purpose. What I hear most often from business professionals who seem deflated after giving an important speech, presentation, or media interview is that they knew they weren't at their best. The difference between adequate and truly excellent is energy. You have tons of it, so let it work for you. Remember, the most important thing about energy is that when you're "up" and "on," you'll always make a connection with your audience.

Another point I want to make about energy is that ENERGY

IS POWER. There is nothing more seductive than power. We all have it. Some people, however, just forget to turn on the switch.

Get acquainted with *your* energy by exploring the following suggestions. These tips and fun homework assignments are designed to help stimulate your energy, and to assist you in pulling it up instantly. These activities will also teach you how to make full use of your energy, especially when you need it most!

1. Briskly rub your hands together. Feel the heat that's generated after just a few seconds. This is a great warm-up exercise. (Don't forget that you have and *ARE* energy.) All that warmth you feel in your hands is representative of those "particles" of energy being stimulated and released as you "perform." Try to imagine "snowflakes" flying around and throughout your whole being — especially in your fertile mind with its unlimited potential.

2. Now that you've got the physical thing going, begin talking quickly about what you're going to do today. Focus on speaking loudly at first. Then add some speed to that volume. Speak as rapidly and loudly as you can. This will increase your production of mental energy. Doing assignments 1 and 2 will help promote a stronger and brisker pace for both your movements and your thoughts, and they'll get you going. Both of these are great exercises for an *everyday, regular, basic warm-up*. Make them a habit.

3. Here's an energy-building exercise you can do prior to that important speech or presentation. A few minutes prior to being "on" — or making your speech or presentation — step outside in the hall or parking lot if you can. Choose a pathway and begin to pace. Take about 20 or 30 rapid, brisk steps one way, then turn around and go the other. While you're pacing, begin jabbering about your speech or presentation material — the louder the better, if you're brave enough. Walk and talk as quickly as you can. This will get you to a pivotal point, energy-wise, before you hit the "stage."

    How many times have you seen a speaker (or experienced it yourself) get off to a slow start and spend five minutes or more picking up steam? Well, after the first few minutes, forget it. The audience has already departed mentally and gone somewhere else. The point is: As a speaker, you can't afford to "build" to a good energy level. You need to open with it! That's what actors do.

This pacing exercise really works. If you're unable to *physically* get up and pace, take a quiet moment on the dais or podium area and do this exercise mentally. You'll begin to feel yourself getting perkier. What you're doing is stimulating your energy field; you're preparing yourself for the big connection. Take note that you should pursue every connection in your daily business activities using the actor's approach: "This is my *one and only* performance, and I'm going to be great!" That thought alone prompts a spurt of energy!

4. Remember: None of us can resist energy. When your energy level is up, your enthusiasm, selling ability, powers of persuasion, and ability to convince are going to optimally position you with regard to your audience. Here's a fun homework task: Try *not* to be affected by someone with enthusiasm. You may not believe what that enthusiastic person is saying, but notice how easily you're swept away by his or her energy. Next time, put yours out there. Then, and only then, can you get back what you really want.

5. Describe something gigantic. Have someone throw out a suggestion as to an item, any item, so that you can improvise. For instance, let's pretend I asked you to describe the biggest toaster in the world. You'll find that as you do this task, your voice will become louder, and you'll be more physically animated. (In other words, the exercise will automatically boost your energy level.)

    You can also imagine that you are a giant. As you walk through your "village," verbally describe the discrepancy in size between yourself and your surroundings. These two games may seem silly at first, but they really work! If you find yourself getting too wired, too energetic, too "up" before a presentation, you can calm yourself with a series of even, diaphragmatic breaths. You'll soon find that you're in control of your energy, and you'll feel a sense of balance.

6. Now, when you work out physically, you also build energy. Notice the energy gain derived from your regular physical exercise. Now translate that same concept into firing up your mental muscles. Do the mental energy exercises every day or, at a minimum, three times a week. Whatever the frequency of your current physical exercise program, match it with your mental exercise program. Just like with your physical exercise program, the more consistently you perform your mental exercises, the better "energy" shape you'll be in.

7. Make a habit of noticing other people's energy levels. For instance, sit outside the supermarket and study the energy levels of the folks going by. Do they have high power energy, medium, low? When you attend speeches or presentations, closely observe the speakers. Analyze them. Do they have good, strong energy? Are they boring you? Do they seem lifeless or full of zip? Make notes and review them to better understand your observations. Prepare a chart, if you like. Study everyone, and ask yourself: Is their energy high, low, in between, non- existent?

   Next, broaden your study group to include actors in television and films, and begin to rate them, too. Notice how energy levels will fluctuate and vary; for instance, not everyone has the energy level of Jack Lemmon, John Belushi, or Robin Williams. There are others who maintain intense, powerful energy levels, but who demonstrate that energy in a different way, such as Glenn Close, James Woods, or Meryl Streep. The power's still there, but it's more inverted. Look at the work of Steve Martin and Jack Nicholson, who play it both high and low. Danny DeVito is an example of someone who always displays a bold energy field, as does Bette Midler; you can see and feel their energy even when they're silent. Clint Eastwood, Gene Hackman, and Kevin Costner, on the other hand, always emit a more placid type of energy, but it's still very present.

   Pick some of your favorite stars, newscasters, friends, co-workers, and role models, and make a study of their energy output. It will tell you a great deal about your own. It will also help you to appreciate your unique, special, and magnificent gift — your energy. Chances are, you'll conclude that you're not fully utilizing your energy potential.

Many of the actors I coach do some pretty weird things backstage to get their energy up before a performance. One tries to run up a wall; another screams into a mirror; a third pretends to be talking to someone who's across the street; another teams up with a fellow actor and starts a shoving and swearing match; still another starts to deliver all of his lines in a grand Shakespearean style; while yet another (and this is really strange) turns on her blender and tries to imitate the sounds of the various cycles. Maybe you can create your own energy "starter."

8. Pet peeves are a fun energy builder, too. Just stand in front of the mirror and begin to opine on different subjects. For instance, talk about what it feels like when someone cuts in front of you in traffic, or when you're forced to clean up someone else's mess. Do a diatribe on the IRS or a politician you're not happy with! On the more positive side, describe how you would feel and what you would do if you'd won the lottery, gotten a big promotion, or won your dream car. Talk about whatever gets your adrenaline going. This is my favorite energy builder, and it's so simple to do!

9. Last rule: While doing all this, of course — HAVE FUN!

"Oh, boy, am I giving my features a workout!
I wonder if Jane Fonda started this way?"

Chapter 11

MAKING FACES

And Not Getting Sent
to Your Room for It

You've heard the old adage: "The lights are on, but nobody's home." That's a term frequently used to describe boring or lifeless people. Well, I don't know about you, but to me, that's how many a speaker looks standing at the lectern. Words are coming out of the speaker's mouth — we know that, because our ears tell us so — but the face, it's dead! Once again, this is part of the energy thing.

Boooorrrrinnnggg!

I won't spend a lot of time on facial animation, but I want you to. It falls in line with "Miller's" theories regarding energy. So here's the lesson.

We have only two things with which to communicate: our voices and our faces. (Yes, we do use our bodies to transmit messages as well, but not to the same extent.) That being the case, we need to maximize the use of our two main assets. It's one thing to have a great voice, but it's quite another to enhance that voice with some natural and appropriate facial animation — or expression.

Here's something to consider: If your face is immobile while you're speaking, chances are that your voice is monotonic, flat, and lifeless. (You'll hear more about this in Chapter 14, where I discuss self-expression.) Therefore, it's incumbent upon you to work the facial muscles, so that when you're speaking, they'll join with your tone and your attitude to literally illustrate the point you're making.

Now, I'm not suggesting that you overexaggerate the muscles and features of your face. Instead, just use them for expressivity. It's such a great visual experience to watch people who constantly surprise you with the way they convey their message, with the way they change the look of their faces. It can be something as simple as a furrowed brow, squint of an eye, wrinkling of a nose, a mischievous smile, slight cock of the head, or pursing of the lips.

Every great actor relies on the clever use of facial animation. Some actors are broadly animated, like Jim Carrey or Robert De Niro, while others, such as Meryl Streep and Melanie Griffith, are more subtle. Most actors play it somewhere in the middle, like Tom Hanks and Sally Field. But all of them animate to some degree. In fact, you should be able to discern an actor's point of view or attitude by the expression he or she "registers." That's powerful. By the way, actors can do entire scenes with no dialogue; they simply choose a variety of facial expressions to convey their message or messages.

If you really want to make a research project out of it (I love doing this kind of thing), get historical. For instance, you might want to study the magic of Stan Laurel and Oliver Hardy. They still blow me away with their fabulous facial animation. Speaking of the pioneers of film, how about Charlie Chaplin, Harold Lloyd, Hattie McDaniel, or the Three Stooges? There are television greats, too, like Sid Caesar, Red Skelton, and Carol Burnett. Make your own list. Rent some old movies. Watch re-runs. Hell, you could write a thesis on this when you're done! More importantly, though, you'll begin to get in touch with the spirit of your own facial dynamics and the energy they transmit.

Remember: As business professionals, we, too, are performers, so the rules don't change for us. Whether speaking, presenting, being part of a panel, or acting, we're still "on." That means we must try, to the best of our abilities, to use all of our gifts of communication.

Following are several exercises that will increase your level of facial activity, thereby enhancing your appeal for the person, or persons, viewing you — your audience.

1. Stand in front of the mirror and do an exercise we call "Best Feature Forward." As you begin talking out loud, focus on one feature and/or portion of your face. For instance, talk with your eyes for a moment; then switch the intensity and focus to your eyebrows; then your eyelashes; emphasize your forehead next; segue to your nose; talk with your upper lip; now exaggerate the use of your teeth; talk with your chin; now talk with your cheekbones. Next, use every feature, every portion, every muscle of your face as you continue on with your oral discourse. You'll be flabbergasted at how many muscles you have in your face! You'll also be amazed at how changeable and interesting your face can be. This homework assignment is a daily must! And if nothing else, it'll definitely make you laugh!

2. Another fun study in this category is to turn off the sound of a movie and just watch the actors' faces. You should be able to read their moods without the advantage of any sound. (That's why I mentioned silent film actors in the above text. I think they were the masters in this category.)

3. Begin watching people on the job or at group gatherings, meetings, presentations, and speeches; and grade them on their animation. Is it interesting? Appropriate? Do they surprise and delight you? Pretend that you're a director, and describe the changes you'd implement to make their faces more expressive and/or interesting.

4. Study the faces of children. They are so expressive, and tell us so much without using a single word.

5. Videotape yourself. Play the tape back without sound. What do you see? What do you like? What would you change? Tape yourself a second time. Better? Keep going until you're satisfied.

6. Stand in front of the mirror and don't speak; just animate your feelings and attitude. Are you convincing? If you can find a "Miller" buddy, stand in front of them and speak using just your facial expressions. Do they get your message? Take turns. (Incidentally, this is a fun way to work out an uncomfortable confrontation with your significant other!)

7. Put a mirror in front of you while you're on the phone. Watch your face as you speak. Do your expressions vary? If not, your voice (and dialogue) don't either.

8. Charades is always a great group game to play when working on facial animation. It's wonderful because you communicate only with your facial expressions and body language. If you have to play charades alone, do so in front of the mirror; it's still great practice.

9. See if you can make up at least one facial animation exercise of your own. You'll feel proud of yourself.

10. After doing these exercises for a while, test yourself during your next speech. Take a second or two to feel your face move with the words you speak. Noting such progress is reinforcing. Finally, remember that you want to be interesting to those you communicate with, whether it's for one minute, one hour, or more.

11. Make sure you're working out daily. Once your facial movements become conditioned, natural expressions will automatically accompany your dialogue. Like the other basic stage skills, eventually you won't have to think about this one either; it will just happen.

"Miller said to lessen my inhibitions and let it all hang out!"

Chapter 12

Ah, Who Cares!!!

Letting Go and Lessening Your Inhibitions

It's very hard to be ourselves when we're uptight. But to be our true self is to be our best. So we need to find a way to stay relaxed, comfortable, and secure in putting our best self forward. If we're in a state of rigidity, fear, or mental paralysis — or all of the above at once — we're not going to be able to react and respond spontaneously; and the spontaneous mode is the one we want to be in. (More on that in the next chapter.) But let me just mention this: To prepare for that free-flowing state of spontaneity, we must first lessen our inhibitions; we need to learn to let go. But isn't it interesting — and also very unfortunate — that the older we get, the more inhibited, restrained, and in-check we become.

Think about this for a second: We are born without inhibitions. Inhibitions are something we acquire. We pick them up like lint on a wool suit. They cling to us, then stick; and like lint balls, they're hard to shake. We come by inhibitions gradually, like freckles or moles. Haven't you noticed? We wake up one day and discover yet another one; and pretty soon, we have a whole bunch of them. And the longer we live, the more inhibitions we seem to accumulate. The process never stops.

Let's go back to improv actors for a moment. As you already know, improv novices spend time on a variety of stage skills. After mastering these skills, they move on to the "jumping-into-oblivion" stage of study, where they're required to function constantly in a state of the unknown. Here are some examples of what they might be asked to do: Talk like a maple tree; yodel through their noses; sing the "Star-Spangled Banner" backward; bark like an Old English Sheepdog; sing an aria with the only lyric being a word like "tachycardia."

For the improv actors, there's no time to consider whether they know HOW to do any of the tasks I've just described, or even whether the assignments make sense. They just have to give it their best shot. Believe it or not, being able, out of the blue, to carry out the above tasks (not to mention about a bazillion others I didn't name) has nothing to do with knowledge. Instead, it has everything to do with guts and commitment. In other words, the actors must first be willing to let go of their inhibitions, stay with that willingness, and then be courageous enough to plow forward with no assurances of anything — including keeping their dignity intact!

When I was first studying improv, my teacher gave me an important directive: Be willing to risk failure at doing improv in order to succeed at it. Well, I don't like to do something unless I can do it well. For instance, I've had my share of tantrums on the ski slopes; and my children once saw me send a non-symmetrical five-layer cake sailing right across the swimming pool and into a crash-landing beyond. What I've discovered about myself is that I'm not too good at public humiliation. (But, then, I don't know too many people who are.) So as you might guess, achieving an open-minded, free-for-all attitude was a big stretch for me.

My same teacher also told me that I had to abandon "self." Oh boy! But the more I was able to do it, the less inhibited I became. And in that state of complete freedom, I was really able to create. Incidentally, that's what improv players do from the start of a piece to its end: They just create one thing after another, from moment to moment. I finally got so good at the game that on the day I was asked to portray a talking pineapple at a luau, I felt no reluctance whatsoever!

I think one of the keys to staying — or becoming — uninhibited is to remember that being inhibited simply means that we're restrained. Now, most business executives I've met are pretty successful and powerful people who can't bear the thought of being restrained. It makes them feel controlled. And freedom is definitely a big deal in this country — freedom of this, freedom of that. How ironic, then, that so many of us are imprisoned by our own, self-imposed safety zones. We rebel automatically to some perceived threats to our freedom, but then completely submit with regard to others. Remember that great line by Kris Kristofferson in "Bobby McGee": "Freedom's just another word for nothing left to lose..."

Being inhibited when we're trying to be spontaneous is like trying to knit while sitting on our hands. So again, we want to strive to lessen our inhibitions first, if we want to flow naturally, in the mental sense.

During tune-up improv workshops, I always ask my actors to just attempt whatever is asked of them, without worrying about the outcome of their performances. When they finally get to that point in class, they're ready for some great results. They're like ripe fruit on a tree: They're ready to be picked! But once again, it's the getting ready part — the letting go — that's the trick.

To recap, you must stay open, you must be in an unwavering state of willingness, and you must commit to the unknown. If you do, the guts part will just happen without any effort.

Some of the following exercises may seem completely outlandish to you, but I'm asking you to try them nonetheless. They'll facilitate your letting go.

1. Start talking to strangers (in safe venues) even if you don't feel like it. Strike up a conversation about anything!

2. Study children at play. Watch how uninhibited they are! During these periods of study, remember that you, too, were much the same way at one time.

3. Call a high school or college buddy and reminisce about some of the crazy things you did together. You know, the things that were nutty, that you probably should have been caught doing, but somehow weren't!

4. While by yourself, or in front of your family or close friends, get up and make a fool of yourself for 10 seconds. I highly recommend this one; in fact, it's one I insist you do every

day. When doing this exercise, don't plan anything. Just get up and do whatever comes to you at that moment that seems utterly ridiculous.

5. If you're normally a jogger or a walker, occasionally skip instead. There's just something about skipping that releases us. Now, sing while you skip!

6. Go to a football game or other audience participation event (hey, maybe even an improv show!) and get involved. Blurt something out. Yell at the ref. Call the plays! (You can always start out at home in front of the TV and work your way up to live events, if you're really shy.)

7. Have a costume party and come as the most bizarre character you can dream up. You may have noticed that most people take on playful and brazen personas at costume parties. Who would you like to be for a night? Be the person you always wanted to be. Get in character. Stay in character.

8. Move around physically and accompany that physical activity with something verbal. For instance, pretend you're a drill sergeant and whip your troops into shape with loud orders while walking back and forth during that discourse. There is something that opens up your ability to let go when you commit physically.

9. Try to do any one of the following for 20 to 60 seconds. After you've done these, make your own list. This is called the "you are" exercise. Do some every single day!

You are:

- An irate scout leader instructing your youngsters on how to make the fundraiser sale
- A member of the British royal family dressing down the servants for setting the table with a dirty fork
- A lazy television repairperson, talking non-stop to your customer
- A neurotic chef teaching your assistant how to make a salad
- A French artist talking to his still-life prop
- A bombastic lawyer trying to sell the jury on the guilt of chocolate pudding

- A car salesman self conscious about his fingernails
- An overly dramatic race-car driver talking to his pit crew
- A spy passing on information about a suspicious tree leaf
- A politician talking in circles — to himself
- A phobic airline pilot trying to explain to the passengers (over the P.A.) why he's flying at an altitude of 200 feet
- A perfectionistic dressmaker/tailor ripping apart a crooked seam
- A frightened camp counselor explaining the virtues of seeing bears in the woods
- A know-it-all gas station attendant talking to a customer about battery acid
- An Italian baker who's paranoid about stale bread

(Okay, now for your last one, go ahead — just try it!!)

- A talking pineapple at a luau

*"I don't know, Harry, it just hit me.
All of a sudden… I just felt like it!?!?!!!"*

Chapter 13

DON'T THINK – JUST BE

Spontaneity —
Doin' What Comes Naturally

This, my dear reader, is the most important chapter in the "Miller" book.

If improv comedy is the "heart" of the "Miller" message, then spontaneity is what makes that heart beat! In my ExecuProv teaching, I place more emphasis on this one aspect of my training than any other. It's my deeply held belief that if you can master the fine art of just "being," and develop the ability to stay in the moment in *that* state, then you're 90 percent home. At that point, you're the best that you can be, because you're as authentic as you can be. Those of us in your audience love authenticity; it promotes that human connection I keep talking about.

For most of us, though, spontaneity is difficult to come by unless we're in an "I don't care" frame of mind, or in a nonthreatening setting, like with a friend. If there's pressure — and it doesn't take much — this ordinary, everyday, take-it-for-granted, God-given spectacular gift suffers. Spontaneity may be only slightly restricted, or it may disappear altogether. Stumbling over words, or halting their natural flow, is the most common malady among the speaking public.

There are a number of reasons why people stumble and fall, both mentally and verbally, at the most inopportune times. Maybe you can identify with one of the following scenarios:

1. You're fine if you're talking to just one or two people, but a whole group of them? Forget it. Tongue-tied is a euphemism for what actually happens to you.

2. You're not as prepared as you thought you were, so when in a state of anxiety you try to wing it, you come off sounding dyslexic.

3. Since you didn't memorize your material beforehand, you find yourself trying to read it; and when you miss groups of sentences, you get embarrassed. You mouth opens, but no words come out.

4. Someone asks a question you weren't anticipating, and you don't know how to respond to it. Your eyes widen, and you just stare at the questioner for an awkwardly long period of time before something inappropriate finally pops out.

5. You're feeling self-conscious about how you look, because suddenly you're not sure that your socks match; but by the time you've worked through that sinking feeling, you've forgotten what you were talking about.

6. You're so intent on impressing the other party (or parties) that you experience an internal freak-out and go into a mumble or stutter.

7. Your "ex"-something — spouse, boss, friend, client — is in the audience, and you accidently spotted that person while proudly doing the eye contact thing. You feel stunned, maybe even light-headed; you want to eject yourself right through the rafters.

We've all been caught in one or more of these situations! Often, we know all the right things to say, but we can't seem to get them out until much later — after everybody's gone, of course. (Don't you love those agonizing mental replays!) If you can relate to any of this, the rest of the chapter should be of great help to you.

Let's talk about great improv players for a minute. Allow me to provide some insight into how they view spontaneity, how they come by it. Actors like Robin Williams, Phil Hartman, Billy Crystal, Dan Ackroyd — they're all masters of the art of improv, and more specifically, of spontaneity. But that didn't happen overnight for any of them, even the quick-tongued Robin Williams. They've all worked very hard at cultivating it, because they understand that spontaneity is the most important tool available to them in the war of wits on stage. It's the ammunition for their verbal arsenal. (You might argue that they all have such overproductive minds in terms of the ability to "spontanate," but guess what — so do you!)

As seasoned improv players take the stage, they do so knowing that they *must* be in the moment, that they must trust their mouths and minds to work in unison in order to constantly create what's appropriate and necessary. The ability to instantly *react* and *respond* (remember, two of the most operative words in the improv vocabulary) requires a very well-toned spontaneity muscle. If any improv player stops to filter a thought before it departs his or her lips, the scene will be thrown completely out of whack. Neither can a player think ahead or plan dialogue; that's simply against the rules. Alternatively, the player can't lag behind the pace either, even by as little as two or three sentences. They must, as we say in the improv world, "be here now."

When players are consistently, constantly in the "current" state, everything works. That's the state of "doin' what comes naturally;" and in that state, all things have a way of threading together rapidly in a natural sequence. When all players follow a few simple rules, scenes come together as if they were written ahead of time — which they never are. Staying within prescribed boundaries and yet also flying free, each scene seems to have a life of its own.

Most great improv players will tell you that they feel as if they're running after their own minds; that they utter words before they fully grasp the thoughts that preceded them. This may sound confusing, but here's an analogy that may help: You hear an extremely loud noise. Very often, your body jumps in reaction to the noise before your brain has fully registered that a loud noise occurred. It's like that.

It takes a lot of self-confidence and trust to be spontaneous in front of an audience. (You probably know that already.) First, you have to trust yourself. Then you have to trust the others in the scene, or room. Next, you have to let go of your inhibitions enough to step forward and jump off that mental cliff. Finally, you have to have faith that the outcome will take care of itself. Wow! That's a tall order. It can be done, though; with enough practice, it can be done with ease, regularity, and consistency.

See, improv is nothing more than a state of crisis. In our everyday lives, crises are common; we have them constantly. Big ones, little ones. Now, when a big one occurs (like an accident, let's say), we don't stop to analyze the situation or make a list of options. We simply react *without thinking*. We do what's needed at that moment in time, whether it means calling for help, offering assistance, or taking over. In improv, you participate in all of the above. You *ARE* 911. So you can see why I say that improv relies on spontaneity.

If it sounds arduous, don't despair. At times, this spontaneity thing is hard for even some of the most seasoned improv players to pull off — to let go, to stay in the moment, to rely on instinct, to react and respond. The inability to respond spontaneously in all circumstances can be traced to a single cause: fear. That's all it is. Think about the times you weren't able to be spontaneous. I'm willing to bet you were blocked by some fear at those moments.

One of my most influential mentors (even to this day) is Gary Austin, founder of the L.A. Groundlings. He agreed to work with my group of actors for a show one night, offering to guest host and lead the actors through the improv pieces. Gary is so highly revered — a legend in his own time — that my actors were mortified. I'll never forget what he told them.

He talked to them about the great Del Close, a famous director and teacher of The Second City improv comedy troupe based in Chicago, and with whom Gary himself had studied. According to Gary, Del always told his students to literally shake their heads free of any fears just before going on stage, and to take out on stage with them the "screw it" adjustment (he used a stronger word than "screw") — in other words, to just not give a damn. Del contended that the mental state of "not caring" made it possible for actors to stay loose, free, uninhibited, and natural (spontaneous), thus enabling them to respond quickly and brilliantly to one another on stage. There's something about *NOT* caring that frees us in everything, isn't there?

As I mentioned previously, spontaneity is nothing more than being genuine, being real, being authentic. For must of us, behaving spontaneously in a business setting requires great skill and a willingness to take risks. We need to be mentally agile in order to respond quickly, and we also have to lessen our inhibitions. Therein lie the twin challenges.

Most people would like to be able to transfer the sense of ease they feel around their loved ones over to the workplace setting, but find they can't do it. Or at least they say they can't. I maintain that we all can, with enough practice.

What's the difference between the dialogue you use when hanging out with your best friend and the way you talk while on the job? With friends and family you don't bring a script with you; you just shoot from the hip verbally. For instance, a friend or family member says something; you say something that goes with their something; then they say something back that relates to your something; you play off that, and so it goes. But in the work "place" — be it a meeting, speech, presentation, or anything in that genre — you tend to get rattled, distracted, defensive, withdrawn, or stay too closely glued to a script. How can you possibly be yourself? How can you be spontaneous? And the problem is that if you're not being yourself, people will know it; and the impression they form of you will be very different from who you *really* are. Talk about mixed messages!

Here's an insight: Residing within your ability to "spontanate" is a great deal of honesty. There's a lot of appeal in that.

And here's something else I'd like you to consider. Most of us don't have a script when we wake up in the morning; that is, we don't begin the day with pages of dialogue listing everything we're going to say until we go to bed that night. Instead, we improvise most of what we say over the course of the day! Maybe some exchanges aren't as comfortable as others, but for the most part we are winging it. My question is: WHY CAN'T WE DO THAT WHEN WE'RE UNDER THE GUN GIVING THAT BIG PRESENTATION, THAT BIG SPEECH????!!! And my theory is: Because we're not trained for it.

I'm not saying that everybody fits this description, but about 90 percent of the people I work with have some phobia about open mental spaces. They feel like they're in the middle of nowhere and don't know where to turn; so they sit in that cerebral desert and wait to be rescued. They sit there in silence as opportunities to say great things pass them by like speeding cars.

The highly trained improv professionals, on the other hand, are never just wandering around the insides of their heads. They're never at a loss for words. They're so well-conditioned that words pop out, at the right time, right place, every time, just like toast from a toaster. But these improv professionals have been primed — drilled even — so that they can deliver under the most arduous and stressful of circumstances. For them, it started long ago when they went away to mental boot camp. In the workshops where they studied, they were made to run the mental marathon so often that going on stage to run the mental mile was like a cake walk.

In doing their job, improv players don't get a head start, like you and I sometimes do; that is, they don't have the benefit of preplanning. They take the stage, and the audience tells them who they are, where they are, what they're doing, and what their conflict or issue is. That's it. From there, using all the information that's provided, the improv players create a scene that has a credible beginning, middle and end. Improv players thrive on the challenge; for them, the thrill of not knowing until the last second is like mental bungee jumping. True, all improv players are on the same page in that they have set guidelines, premises, and rules to go by (like great jazz players who have the structural foundation of a strong classical background); but still, they don't have a clue as to what will happen in any scene until it happens. They make it work, because they know there's no bailing out. And most importantly, like great prizefighters, they WORK OUT continuously to stay in shape so that their efforts always reap rewards. You can ask any improv player who's had to miss one or two sessions of class, and they'll tell you they feel a little rusty.

This is true for the rest of us as well. If we never work out, our spontaneity muscle will atrophy. If we use it only occasionally, it may support us only some of the time. So your goal (and mine) is to become so mentally "buff" that you can be spontaneous with ease, even when you're under pressure. With regular workouts, a quick wit and appropriate responses become as automatic as breathing.

After years of teaching improv comedy techniques to business executives, I'm even more firmly convinced that improv basics are the key to great speaking, presentation, and communication skills. I don't care how good you think you already are; you can't plan for every eventuality. Because of that, you must be able to fall back on your ability to be spontaneous.

Curiously enough, when a speech is well rehearsed, and the speaker is well trained, the overall impression is of something that was *not* rehearsed. We in the audience perceive the presenter as smooth and conversant; we feel like he or she has been talking directly to us, rather than talking at us. Very few business people are this practiced, however; and when they "try" to make us believe that they are, we figure it out anyway. We're too smart to be tricked like that.

In working with my students, I always encourage them to prepare the type of speech or presentation that appears to be spontaneous. I'd prefer that my students take their written speech and just paraphrase it using *their* own words; or take just an outline, or the essence of their message, and deliver that spontaneously. (This process is covered in Chapter 21, The "Square Within A Square Theory.") Why do I say that? Because the end result is always better. Their listeners are more comfortable, and my students aren't spending all their time and energy trying to recall content. Rather, they can focus on the real reason they're there — to talk to the audience in their own words, in their own way.

If you have the self-discipline to memorize and rehearse your material, bully for you; I'd like to meet you. But if you're like most of us, you don't have sufficient time or interest in that kind of preparation. The next best thing, then, is to develop your spontaneity muscle and use it. Believe it or not, it's not that difficult. And you have a head start over even the most seasoned improv player: You have some idea of what's to come. You're certainly not going to get up and talk about something you know nothing about. You have your present job because you're good at it, and that means you must be knowledgeable. So in some ways improvising should be easier for you than for the improv player. Given that, just do a reasonable amount of mental preparation, and then speak from the heart. Your audience will love it!

What I find most intriguing about spontaneity is this: The more spontaneous you are, the more spontaneous you become. I know from past experience that when I'm writing comedy, just flinging one thought after another, my mind keeps escalating to levels of greater and greater creativity. The higher the level, the more spontaneous I become; the more spontaneous, the more lucid, more prolific, etc. I think when we're able to be completely free (but still on track with our purpose), we can say and do genius-like things.

It's been my experience that when a speaker knows the subject matter and just takes off with it, he or she is more convincing; and I'm more easily sold. But when a speaker stays on book (uses a script), he or she often bogs down. (Besides, I hate looking at the tops of speakers' heads when they speak, don't you?)

If you forget everything else in this chapter, I'm asking you to remember this one thing: When you "try" to be a certain way, that implies that you're expending energy; you're working at it. It's hard to be natural in that state. To "be" is just that. You just "are." In fact, you can take a cue from nature. A rose doesn't try to be a rose; it just is one. So don't force it. Just roll with it, as Steve Winwood would say.

Remember, if you can speak, you can be spontaneous. You can follow your instincts. You can go with the flow. You can play off your audience, and deliver a speech or presentation that's appropriate — right there, right then. You can react quickly and appropriately in all circumstances, even the tough ones related to your job.

I'm definitely *not* suggesting that you go into a speech or presentation without preparing for it. You should do as many run-throughs as you feel necessary. In other words, do your research, know your subject matter, and be organized. What I am recommending, however, is that you let it flow when you get up in front of the audience.

Here's a good example of what I've been talking about. One of my clients is a major trucking company that I've worked with for a long time. They called me one day and asked me to coach them on a major presentation they were making to Federal Express. When I met with the six members of the team making the pitch, I asked them to run their presentation by me so I could see what they had. Well, what they had was 90 minutes of materials — overheads, graphs, etc., etc. I had to control myself to keep from yawning.

After some discussion with my client, I learned that Fed Ex was sending six of its people to the presentation, but that my client didn't know what information these people wanted, so my client had decided to just give them everything they had. We huddled. I recommended that they give the Fed Ex team ten to 15 minutes of history, background, and company capability, and leave the rest of the time for open discussion. If Fed Ex asked a question about routes and access points, my client could then address that issue using a visual backup and an expert from the team. And by playing off Fed Ex's questions, my client could get a better sense of what Fed Ex wanted from the process, and subsequently furnish them with the answers that related directly to their "then and there" needs and concerns.

They did it; it worked. Every member of my client's team knew his or her stuff, so that when the proverbial ball came their way, they were able to competently improvise their answers. One reason the process proved so successful (in addition to providing Fed Ex with precisely the information they needed from the presentation) is that the spontaneity strategy allowed for some real bonding between the two teams. They had a chance to get to know each other during that 90-minute session, and there was a real sense of connection. As a result, by the time the meeting came to a conclusion, the dominant mood in the room was one of camaraderie.

One more real-life example before I get to your homework. When my acting company does an improv show, I moderate for the cast. What that means is that I take the stage between sketches and improv pieces, and ask the audience for "set ups," for input to be used in the show; and I chat with the audience. Since every night and every audience is different, I can't say the same things week after week. I have to be in the moment; I have to be mentally agile so I can be spontaneous.

Both the audience and I have fun. It always works. There's no trick. I just react and respond to what's going on right there, right then. I stay firmly in the moment throughout the verbal exchange. I use my weekly performances as a regular spontaneity workout. There are times, I'll admit, when it's still a little uncomfortable; I never know what's going to happen. Fortunately, the constant repetition reinforces my confidence in my ability to handle just about anything!

To summarize what I've covered so far, the key to achieving spontaneity (particularly under pressure) is to first develop self-trust; then lessen your inhibitions; find ways to keep yourself mentally agile; and, finally, stay in the moment.

One of the first things I want you to do is to study children between the ages of three to seven years, which are the most spontaneous ages. Notice how quick and agile these children are in terms of thoughts, moods, expressions, ideas, and questions. Just sit and watch them at play, especially when they're playing by themselves. The reason they are so loose is because at those ages, they have no inhibitions. We, on the other hand, are full of them — imposed by society, our life experiences, confining lifestyles, fear, and habit.

The trick, then, is to get back to your beginnings, to plop yourself down in the midst of the spontaneity you demonstrated as a kid. I think we can agree that there are times, even as an adult, that you're in a natural and authentic state of being; but when it would get you the most mileage, you probably have a tendency to stay with what feels safe. By that I mean that rather than your mind feeling like it's the playing field of the L.A. Coliseum, it's more like it's locked inside a Volkswagen trunk. When we're too confined, we shut down. Those mental electrode currents just aren't firing, so we end up brain dead. Well, I'm asking you to take some risks from this point forward.

Chin up! It's time to retrain. It's time to stop thinking so much, to stop managing, modulating, filtering, analyzing, considering, weighing, controlling. It's time instead to just let go and be. Know your subject matter, get organized. Then take flight.

While most spontaneity exercises are done in teams of two or more, I've designed some that you can do either with or without another person. The most important recommendation I can make is that you do the exercises daily in order to build that mental muscle of spontaneity.

1. Try the Flashcard exercise, which goes like this: Have someone you know write down nouns on pieces of paper, like the flashcards used by schoolchildren. Then have the other person flash these cards at you for just a few seconds each time. When you see the noun, start talking about that subject as fast as you can. Don't repeat the written word when you start thinking about it, though; that only gives you time to stall and think. The idea is to not think, but instead to just gab away.

   If you don't have a flashcard buddy, just go somewhere (it can even be in the car on the way to work) and start talking about different objects you see. As soon as your eye catches something, start on that subject. And so forth. You want to go as fast as you can without staying on any one thing for any length of time. The more often you change your focus from one thing to another, the more agile your mind becomes.

2. Have someone write down the first line of a story. Maybe you have children, a significant other, or someone you can rely on to feed you sentences each day. If you live alone, ask a co-worker to make up a batch of sentences for you that will last a week or two. Now, stand in front of the mirror, read a sentence (one a day), and make up a story from there. Continue with the story for three to five minutes. This enhances your creativity, as well as your spontaneity and mental agility.

3. This exercise is similar to the one above, but this time, the sentence you read will be your closing sentence, your punchline, whatever you want it to be, just so long as it comes at the end of your story. Now, make up a story or a joke that *leads* up to that last sentence. Once again, you'll be pleasantly surprised at how capable you are, not only of building to that finish, but also of cleverly making sense on your way *to* that finish line.

4. Expert Talker is fun! Have someone make up a non-existent word, or take a word and spell it backwards. Make it a long one, or at least three syllables. First, you must pronounce it. Then, pretending it's your field of expertise, stand up and

begin talking about your profession — explain what it is, how you became an expert in it, what you do as expert so and so. If the opportunity arises, do this in front of an audience, and have them ask questions of you afterward.

Some examples of professions might be: a Ribernort; a Pullicist; a Dorflam; a Borscart; a Flibaurgrapher; a Misimgstrortflat; or an Ethingarphologist. If you have children over the age of seven or eight, they will have a ball helping you with this one. When you do take the "podium" in this exercise to begin your discourse as an "expert," be sure to speak with strong stage skills and a great deal of conviction and confidence. Really make yourself and/or your audience believe you are whatever you profess to be.

5. Try a one-minute commercial. Take an object — for example, a hairbrush. Now, decide that it is anything but what it really is. (In other words, it *can't* be a hairbrush.) Next, announce the name of your product, tell your audience (or yourself in the mirror) what it is, what it will do for you, how it works, where you can get one, how much it costs, and your slogan. You have only one minute to do this exercise. This is one you can do everyday, and it'll provide you with a good mental stretch.

6. This is another one for which you'll need assistance. Have someone write down categories of things, like ice cream, cars, resorts, mystery books, etc., and place these slips of paper in an envelope. Now, as you pull each category from the envelope, you'll need to name three things that fit within that category; for example, Vanilla, Rocky Road, and Chocolate "ice cream." Do it fast and furiously; that's when it becomes challenging. Make sure someone will help you with this one; if you make up your own categories, you can cheat. If you cheat, what's the point?

7. Take a certain time of day at work and find someone to converse with. What I want you to do is to just focus on being as spontaneous as possible during your part of the conversation, with your dialogue, even if you had previously planned what you wanted to say. Let the other person dictate the course of the conversation; just play off that dia-

logue with whatever feels instinctively appropriate. The results may astound you!

8. Graduating from the last exercise, see if you can participate in a meeting more spontaneously than you normally would. Have your reports or materials ready, but see if you can go with the flow of what feels natural when you impart the information. Don't be formal or "corporate." Stay human, be spontaneous. See what happens.

9. Make a concerted effort to find an opportunity to speak in front of a group. (Maybe you do this every day anyway, so finding the right situation may be easy for you.) Have your pitch or speech ideas with you, but see if you can improvise your message and/or ideas. Create other opportunities to do this as often as possible. This will serve to condition you to be more impromptu. If you start out with small, less meaningful presentations, you can then graduate to bigger, more important ones.

10. If you don't do so already, the next time you make a speech, set aside time for a question and answer period. This forces you to be spontaneous, and it's great practice in confronting the unexpected with poise and confidence. As an added incentive, the more you interface with your audience, the better your chances for connecting with them.

11. Make sure you do something spontaneous twice a day, once in the morning and once in the afternoon. Keep a log of what you did. List any comments on how you felt and the reactions you received. Forcing yourself to engage in spontaneous activity everyday should be part of your ongoing regimen. Soon, that regular program will become — you guessed it — spontaneous! Eventually, you'll opt for being spontaneous rather than scripted when it comes to those speeches and what used to be "canned" presentations. In the process, everything will become that much more interesting to you and, of course, to your audience as well.

12. If you're a salesperson or customer service representative, or do some type of job that requires verbal repetition, make it a part of your daily routine to handle every call, every

customer, *differently*. Rearrange your dialogue. Add something new. The goal is to do something, anything, differently from one call to the next. Be spontaneous as you go about making those changes.

What you'll notice is that you are increasingly more interested in what you're saying because your material is suddenly fresher. This can't help but make a positive impact on the "receiver" of your information or pitch. Many of us are required to do the same presentation over and over. This is especially true of salespeople, instructors, and speech-givers. Broadway actors, incidentally, must do the same show sometimes six days a week for years. They work very hard to give every performance something new.

You may find other ways in which to promote your unique gift of spontaneity. There are no limitations in this area of study. The only guidelines are: Don't think; just be.

"It's not **what** I say but how I say it...
and how I look when I say it that gets my point across."

Chapter 14

WHAT DO YOU MEAN?

The Act of Expressing Yourself

Words, words, words. You've heard one, you've heard them all. At least that's how it sounds from the mouths of some people. There's nothing more boring than listening to a voice that has no inflection, no intonation, no meaning to go with the words that are being spoken; a voice that drones on for infinity. God help us!

You've heard these people. They sound like they're reading ingredients for a recipe, or instructions on how to put something together — when in actuality they're making a major speech on motivation or something totally incongruent like that! Their delivery sounds like this: First you put the...then you add the...next you put the...then you add the...We feel like running screaming into the night. And very often these same people will say things like "It sure is a nice day," or "Wait until I show you our new product," or "Your house is on fire." What's frightening is all of those statements sound the same.

Such people suffer from what I call "self-expressionlessness." Although it's not a terminal presentation disease, it is serious — grave enough, in fact, to ensure that these people will seldom, if ever, get the results they're aiming for.

I have a theory that underlying every supposedly analytical decision is an impulse that actually drives it, an emotional trigger that makes us react or respond to the "seller." I don't want to get into the Madison Avenue psychology of clever advertising campaigns and slogans, or political speech writing; the point is, though, that many of these ads are carefully crafted to cause us to "act."

They motivate us; they make us yearn, make us want. But what we're reacting to is not WHAT they're saying; it's HOW they're saying it.

What I'm referring to here is the energy and expression that support the written word. (When you speak, think of the "meaning" being expressed as a buttress that supports a bridge.) Listen to radio commercials or to certain political figures.

Jesse Jackson is a good (but somewhat extreme) example; he really gets his message across by using a good deal of emotion. An even better example is John F. Kennedy. He was a master at this, because during his speeches, press conferences, or just about any time he spoke, he took his listeners along for a "ride." He ran the gamut from genuine concern to compassion to humor — he played the emotional field eloquently and knowingly. I'm sure you can think of others who fit into this category. They don't have to be celebrity types either; they're just everyday people who express themselves well.

My point is that speakers, presenters, and salespersons can elicit a strong emotional reaction from others when they push various emotional buttons. And it's not the words they're using that push these buttons; it's how the words are delivered.

The "how" of delivery includes intonation. Interestingly enough, the meaning of a word can change depending on the intonation we give it. For example, if I say "I really like your shoes" using a sarcastic tone of voice, that will have one meaning for you; but if I say the same sentence in a sincere manner, I will have imparted an entirely different message. To hear what I mean, try that same sentence using different moods, such as "nervous," "silly," "sexy," "angry," and so on. I think you'll be amazed at the results!

In improv comedy workshops there's an exercise we do called "Lock In Your Lines." In this exercise, three people start to make up a scene. They're instructed to use short, easy-to-remember sentences in improvising their dialogue, because they'll be asked to repeat the scene verbatim several times.

They're given suggestions, too, such as a place to be and a conflict. They're asked to first deliver the lines without any emotion or attitude — to just speak the words. Later, we assign various emotions and attitudes.

In a recent exercise, the place was a restaurant, with two actors playing customers and the third a waiter; and the conflict was cold food. From there the three players improvised the scene, which lasted about one minute. After the three had run through the scene several times and "locked in their lines," they were then required to repeat it, this time varying the mood of the scene based on suggestions from the audience. Whatever mood the audience suggested, all three players were required to maintain that same, identical mood throughout the scene. This was very funny to watch, and also made an important point: Each time a new mood was introduced, the scene took on a completely different meaning. That's why the gospel according to "Miller" is: "*It's not what you say; it's how you say it!*"

Here's an example of the "Miller" gospel at work. You know how sometimes you see (and hear) speakers you admire, but you're not sure why they appeal to you; they just do. They just seem to have some magical thing that grabs you — you and everyone else in the room, too. Your mind doesn't wander; you're there to stay. Such speakers are often described as having charisma.

Well, I believe that everyone has the potential to be charismatic. No, really; it's true! Charisma is nothing more than a good personality, and a good personality is nothing more than a natural and free-flowing ability to self-express. Great speakers and presenters don't trudge verbally along in the same one or two moods throughout their presentations; instead, they constantly change moods to fit the meaning of what they're attempting to convey.

You see, if you don't punch up your words with meaning and a variety of emotions, you won't "hook" the listener. And if you don't hook the listener, you won't make the all-important human connection. The end result? The job doesn't get done, and you know what that means: You won't sell your "thing," whatever it is.

Here's something to ponder: One of the reasons most of us

can sit through movies for two hours without growing restless, without thinking about work, our personal problems, or the world in general, is because we're so captivated by the performers in the film. An exciting, colorful story helps, too, of course; but without believable and all-expressive characters, we would just tune out.

And yes, we've all seen some pretty boring, one-mood kind of actors. (Without meaning to offend anyone, I'd put John Wayne in this category; I'm sure you can think of others.) On the other hand, look at Robert de Niro, Meryl Streep, Jack Nicholson, and so many other laudatory contemporary actors. What is it about them that you enjoy? My guess is, if you were to sit back and really analyze them, you'd find that each has a fabulous way of self-expressing. Nicholson, for example, is a great study, because he changes moods so rapidly and surprisingly. In fact, there are times when I'd swear he's doing two or three emotions simultaneously. This is what keeps us riveted to the screen when we watch him.

Check out the people around you — speakers, people who talk at meetings, your co-workers — and identify those you find fascinating. Look, too, at the people you're attached to, and the people you relate to easily and feel comfortable about approaching. I'm willing to bet that they're able to express themselves with ease. I'm also willing to bet that they put meaning behind their words, and do so with believability.

After coaching so many clients, and introducing them all to various "emotional" exercises, I've come to realize that the ability to self-express is the major factor — the key, really — in helping my clients to attain their maximum power and effectiveness as speakers. I've also come to appreciate that every person (barring any major speech impediment or deep emotional disturbance) has the ability to *SAY* what he or she really means. If that's the case, you might wonder why people need instruction in something that should come automatically.

Well, I've explored that, too, and here's what I came up with. When we were children — let's say four or five years old — we just said whatever popped into our little minds. If we wanted something, most often we just said so. If we didn't like something, we let that be known, too. Rarely, at that age, did we go within and hide our feelings. However, as we grew older, we got some very specific messages like "Don't cry, or I'll give you something to cry about;" "If you can't say anything nice, don't say anything at all;" "Get that look off your face;" and my personal favorite, "Don't talk to strangers." (Chew on that one for a minute. Could it have anything to do with your reluctance to speak in front of a group of people you don't know?) So we began to hesitate a little about speaking up and/or out —in effect, we hesitated to express ourselves.

As we got older, we began to guard our feelings. Rather than responding, we'd withdraw from certain situations, especially in high school (the shutdown capital of our youth). And we got very familiar with the damage that only the world around us could inflict.

Once we hit the workplace and began to experience some success and/or rejection as business professionals, we opted for taking as few chances as possible; we chose NOT to be at risk, but instead to keep our thoughts and FEELINGS to ourselves (uh-oh, might say the wrong thing!). One consequence of that self-protection, though, was that our speeches, presentations, and overall communication became somewhat restricted, constrained, stilted, and eventually, bland. We have stopped expressing ourselves — in some cases almost completely.

Something intriguing I've learned from observing my clients is that the more successful they are, the more withdrawn and emotionally shut down they seem to be. When I ask about this, they confide that they're afraid of losing their positions, the ones they worked so hard to get. Men and women in their 40s and 50s seem to be the most affected. They've made it to the top, and don't want to risk blowing it by saying the wrong thing; the distance to the bottom — the fall — is too great. In general, it seems that younger people, with less to lose perhaps, are more apt to express their opinions and feelings. But with older people, well, as one client put it, "It's better for me to live inside this safe little box than to venture out into the unknown."

I've suggested previously that you observe four- and five-year olds. Now, as a comparison, take a look at some 75-year plus individuals. Many of them are so shut down that they've literally rolled up into a ball, kind of bent in half, fetal-like. You can see the pain. And I'm not referring to physical pain; I mean the toll taken on the body by emotional suppression.

I firmly believe that if you work every day on keeping your emotions alive and at the forefront, you'll be much better prepared to express yourself when you really want something. I tell my students to think of their work in this area as expanding their "emotional" vocabulary. The analogy I use is that of a well, and my students' emotions are buried underneath the dirt at the bottom of this well. If they keep pulling up these emotions and expressing them fully, soon the feelings will float up to where the water meets the air. There the emotions will sit, ready and able, just like a water skier, to pop up and take off! Eventually, with enough working out, the ability to express the meaning behind the words will become automatic and spontaneous, just like with young children.

Performers know the value of working out in this way. They spend hours experiencing different "feelings" in order to add dimension, interest, credibility, and believability to their characters; they're constantly exercising their emotional muscles. What's pertinent about the way good actors study is that they work very hard at having their emotional expression be truly authentic.

When I work with my students at the comedy school, I always tell them, with respect to emotional exercises, to live the emotion from THE INSIDE OUT. Many bad actors, as well as business professionals who are feigning emotion (and this is common among salespeople), tend to live it from THE OUTSIDE IN. They emote, but there's no truth in their attempts. It just doesn't work. People won't ever be sold by a sales pitch that seems contrived, phony or false. Try to remember this "Miller" adage when you think about self- expression: "If you believe it, they'll believe it." The emotion has to come from within; it has to be real.

Something you might not realize about self-expression is that the ability to express yourself is a form of entertainment. And as a speaker, your number one job is to entertain your audience. The best way to do that is to take them all over the emotional map with your delivery. If you incorporate a broad range of moods or emotions, you'll always captivate your listeners.

On the other hand, if your entire speech is delivered using just one or two moods — say enthusiastic and serious — then after a while, your audience will tune you out (like an airplane engine; first you hear it, then you don't). Your audience will perceive you as boring and predictable; and there's no entertainment value in that. So remember to vary your moods while speaking.

Here's another "Miller" precept with regard to delivery: "It's contrast and variety that make us interesting." In addition to diversifying your emotional delivery — what I call "mood variance" — you should also vary the volume and speed of your voice. Your voice can be soft, then loud, then normal; it can be fast, then slow, then staccato. There are many ways to maintain your audience's interest level. Remember, though, that the emotional segues are by far your most powerful tool.

When you engage people with energy and self-expression, they can't resist you. They'll really hear your message. And they won't forget you either. You'll make that all- important impression, then the human connection, and quite possibly a "sale," too. It's hard to say no to a person who's fully expressed himself or herself. For example, just try to say no to your small children or grandchildren the next time they want a certain toy, ice cream cone, or whatever. When they really get behind what they want, it's hard to refuse them.

If you're truly expressive and sincere, it will be hard for anyone to refuse you either. Now that you're fairly well convinced that self- expression is a major tool in becoming a great communicator, you'll want to know how to tap into yours. Well, the following homework assignments are guaranteed to raise your level of self-expression and give you back the gift that you were born with! But if you don't do the exercises regularly and seriously, you may slip right back into that monotonous, one-emotion groove. For those of you who already consider yourselves to be highly self-expressive, do these exercises anyway; you'll only get better. One final suggestion: Do them at your own pace. This is not parochial school!

1. At the end of the chapter you'll find a long list of moods and emotions. Read each of the following sentences every

day using at least 10 different emotions until you've covered the entire list. Sometime in the future, add moods and emotions that are not listed here.

- I can't stand her. I really can't stand her.
- I'm going to the store. I'll be back later.
- I've got a business meeting scheduled this morning.
- Where are you going?
- I already made plans for the weekend.
- We finally got a new puppy.
- I had spaghetti for lunch yesterday.
- I've never been happy.
- I haven't got time for that right now.
- She really shouldn't have done that.

Note how the meaning changes according to the emotion used. After you've done the sentences, graduate to a paragraph out of *The Wall Street Journal*. Now, read that in several different moods. If there's a mood on the list that you don't recognize, look it up in the dictionary (and don't feel bad about doing that). It's very common for my students to realize they don't know the meaning of the "feeling" they're attempting to convey.

2. Read aloud to children. Really express the characters as you read the dialogue. Change your voice — tone, volume, dialect, FEELING — as you read the words for each character. Children love this, and you'll find it less threatening to really express in their presence (as opposed to other adults). You can experiment safely.

3. Do the walk-and-express exercise. Here's how it goes: Walk forward, counting from one to ten, in a specific mood. When you count, let the mood build to a peak. By the time you reach the number ten, you should be at the height of expressing that particular mood. Now, walk backwards, letting the mood go from ten to nine to eight, etc., until the mood subsides and is expressed only quietly as you reach the number one.

4. Make yourself some flashcards, and write down one emo-

tion or mood on each card. Shuffle the cards. Start your practice speech or presentation using an "emotional" card to dictate your mood. Surprise yourself by flipping over a new "emotional" card every few sentences, and then putting that emotion behind your dialogue. Just flow with it, even though your speech material may seem incongruent with the mood listed on the card. Remember, the contrast can be very interesting. Try it.

5. Try reciting nursery rhymes in various moods. The content is easy to remember, and this helps you concentrate fully on the mood you're trying to express. For example, try "Mary Had A Little Lamb" in anger, then in compassion, and so on.

6. Do the implode/explode improv exercise, which goes like this: Pick a mood. Start talking explosively in that mood — just really let go. Then, staying in the same mood, pull it in, pull it back, and express it more quietly. This exercise allows you to explore varying levels of intensity.

7. Study various actors. Ask yourself what they did in a particular scene to evoke a response in you. Write down your answers. Run that scene again on your VCR. It will help you analyze what "mood variance" really means.

8. Look into the mirror and, without making a sound, express an assigned mood or emotion using facial expressions. Do this with your eyes, then just your nose, focus on your mouth, now your cheekbones, next your forehead, etc. (Best Feature Forward, remember?) Can you see the attitude or mood registered in your facial expression? Now, make a guttural sound (no words) that expresses that feeling. Then relax your face, and try another mood.

9. Try talking gibberish (unintelligible words). The idea is to express your meaning using intonation rather than words. You can deliver your whole speech in gibberish just to get in touch with the intent behind the words. A great adjunct to this is to address a willing friend in gibberish, and see if that friend can figure out what you're trying to communicate. If you can get your point across under these circum-

stances, then you've really mastered the "emotional" game!

If you do your homework a couple of times a week, mood variance will become automatic to you, like drying your hands or opening the cupboard; you won't have to think about *how* to do it. You won't have to try to get meaning to support your words, or to think about the mood you want to convey. Your words will just come out naturally and with a lot of conviction.

Suggested Moods and Emotions

Candid	Cantankerous	Opinionated
Dizzy	Mischievous	Pained
Scared	Fiery	Feeble
Dismal	Forceful	Shocked
Evasive	Pitiful	Indecisive
Hopeless	Sharp	Tricky
Ecstatic	Shrewd	Alluring
Prudish	Impassioned	Inferior
Lonesome	Bewitching	Pompous
Innocent	Envious	Nervous
Withdrawn	Self-conscious	Concerned
Crude	Perplexed	Tired
Guilt-ridden	Winsome	Catty
Effeminate	Immature	Conceited
Worried	Wistful	Lovesick
Overwhelmed	Engrossed	Sweet
Giddy	Haggard	Heartbroken
Sprightly	Shifty	Bitter
Childlike	Defensive	Comical
Violent	Scorned	Arrogant
Carefree	Self-important	Capricious
Honest	Insulted	Regal
Energized	Vulnerable	Frivolous
Self-centered	Excited	Positive
Stressed	Confident	Neurotic
Skeptical	Elated	Casual
Philosophical	Deceptive	Pensive

Genuine	Angry	Passionate
Happy	Macho	Desperate
Grateful	Shy	Dumb
Intellectual	Silly	Superior
Fearful	Resentful	Surprised
Melancholy	Anxious	Confused
Worried	Bored	Sentimental
Depressed	Complex	Compassionate
Delighted	Longing	Mysterious
Amazed	Seductive	Delirious
Mystical	Spiritual	Negative
Disgusted	Argumentative	Powerful
Contrary	Uncontrollable	Discouraged
Laughing	Frustrated	Confident
Aloof	Sarcastic	Wishful
Irritable	Manic	Hostile
Unpredictable	Cynical	Demanding
Loving	Insightful	Shakespearean
Condescending	Lustful	Patronizing
Snobbish	Direct	Serious
Poised	Breathless	Commanding
Smitten	Rude	Impudent
Stubborn	Timid	Uncertain
Indifferent	Appalled	Nauseated
Sleepy	Sexy	Stupid
Insane	Strange	Parental
Cocky	Demure	Touched
Sensitive	Secretive	Aggressive
Patriotic	Hatred	

"Let's see...a one an' a two an' a three..."

Chapter 15

5-6-7-8...IT'S *TIME*
YOU SHOULD APPRECIATE

Establishing and Building Your Sense of Timing

I want you to stop and relax for a minute, and think over the essential messages and lessons you've learned so far. If you stack them up, if you integrate them, you'll begin to see how these puzzle pieces fit together. Even more exciting, you'll understand how applicable these skills are to becoming a more fantastic speaker and communicator. Don't forget: Your job is to entertain!

So, thus far you've worked on basic stage skills, awareness, concentration, eye contact, energy, animation, self-expression, lessening inhibitions, and spontaneity. Now I'm going to add one more ingredient to the performance stew. It's called timing. In this chapter, I hope to teach you several important things about timing: how it's a natural by-product of spontaneity; how important it is to making a good presentation; how it supports your unique style; and how it impacts the effectiveness of the impression you make on your audience.

Everyone has timing.

The first thing you can do to get in touch with *your* sense of timing is to observe the rhythm of your gait when you're walking. That's a great starting point.

When you're spontaneous, you usually display an innate, effortless sense of timing. This is easiest to see when you're just hanging out with your friends, co-workers, family, and children.

There's no pressure in those instances. Think about the times when you're in a relaxed environment, and you're recounting an incident or telling a story, whether humorous or sad. As you do, you hit all the right spots, with all the right words and all the right emotions and all the right pauses at what appear to be all the right places. You hold back a bit on the suspenseful parts; you get louder and faster with the exciting parts; perhaps you become more intense with your delivery as you approach the finish, and you may even complete your story with a big burst of energy. All of these shifts tend to add diversity to the pace of your story-telling. And that is how timing works when you verbalize.

Timing is essential in music, athletics, and theater. In comedy, it's critical. Stand-up comics would bomb without it. Improv players need it, too, since so much of their work relies on pace, cadence, flow. In fact, I think improv actors need good timing more than just about anyone!

When actors study the fundamentals of improv, they're constantly working with timing; so the training is a valuable tool for developing sensitivity to their own timing and that of others. In fact, during the training process, improv actors employ timing in just about every aspect of their work. Good timing is the difference between funny and not funny, between boring and interesting.

If you haven't had the benefit of musical training, then this lesson may be a whole new experience for you. If you have, then you'll appreciate how important that training was, and how you can now transfer that knowledge to your work as a speaker or presenter. If you're a professional musician, or even an amateur, I think you can still learn something from this "Miller" discourse; it may allow you to see timing in a very different light.

I was fortunate to have grown up in a musical family. My father is a jazz bassist; my mother was a singer and, up until her untimely death, a fabulous dancer. My sister is very musically inclined as well; but somehow I couldn't do anything in tune, so I often sat on the sidelines and tapped my foot. By doing so, however, I did develop a well-trained ear; so my family's influence was substantial. I trained my ear by just listening and tapping. My sense of timing showed up in other ways — in my writing and performing.

I was a lyricist for quite a while, and now I write comedy. I know I had a slight edge because of my well-developed ear. For me, good timing seems as ordinary as skiing probably is to the child of a ski instructor. When you grow up with a parent whose life's work involves a specific talent, you tend to come by it rather naturally; so I was lucky. God knows where my timing would be without all that!

Once again, I couldn't sing, but I had a knack for keeping the beat and hearing the intricacies of many musical pieces. It was all around me. I could dance, too, which helped me tremendously in my storytelling as a speaker, and knowing how to get a laugh, when to pause for one, and when to start talking again. All those little touches depend on a trained ear and a sense of rhythm.

Don't confuse rhythm with good intonation. You can work on your musicality without being able to sing in tune, for instance, or play an instrument. In other words, movement and sound are independent of one another. Movement is rhythm. To be a good speaker, all you need is rhythm. So if you can't sing in tune or play an instrument, who cares. I can't sing either (as much as I want to). That has nothing to do with being a good speechmaker; but timing sure does.

I'm sure you know people who are great at telling stories and eliciting laughs or evoking dramatic reactions from their audiences. If you analyze them, they're probably also the people who seem to be spontaneous, confident, and very much at ease at the podium.

It's very difficult to think tempo when you're uptight, by the way. When you're under pressure, your timing is one more thing that goes — just goes out the window like a well-thrown Frisbee. It's also very tough to force timing. It can't be done; it has to ebb and flow. It has to be indigenous to you.

If you're musical then, I'm asking you to take all you know about music and apply it to speaking. Think about timbre, phrasing, pitch, rhythm, syncopation. Are you in concert (pardon the pun) with any of these elements when you *present*? Maybe you thought these concepts only related to singing or playing a musical instrument, but they don't. Bolstering your speaking style with musical accoutrements is very effective. My favorite speakers are the ones who tell good stories; and those speakers all have that great "ear" going for them!

In ExecuProv training, we put a lot of emphasis on exercises that improve timing. We call them "keening up the ear." Some of our drills are listed at the end of this chapter. I urge you to include them in your regular workouts.

So besides becoming aware of your "walk," as I mentioned earlier in this chapter, you can also get in touch with the concept of timing by listening to sounds. I mean *really* listening. Everything has a rhythm. Many sounds we hear continually throughout the day are rhythmic, including the dishwasher, car engine, leaky faucet, adding machine, creaking door — the list goes on. You can pretty much count on the fact that anything mechanical, repetitive, or constant has a rhythm. So begin by listening intently to the regularity of sounds, whether the source is man-made or natural.

Next, begin to listen to the difference between your delivery in a casual setting and your delivery during a speech or presentation. I want you to first identify the characteristics of your timing in the casual setting. Take note of your phrasing (that's particularly important), notice where the pauses are, and gauge your tempo. Are these characteristics also present in the more formal atmosphere? If they are, then you're probably in sync with yourself most of the time and already using your gifts.

On the other hand, if there's a marked discrepancy in your delivery between the two settings (i.e., when relaxed, you're okay, but in the formal setting you're running sentences together, speaking staccato — anything that indicates nervousness), then you need to work on perfecting your timing. It will carry you when you're under pressure. Good timing can actually make a performance, and that's why I want you to master it. Then you'll be able to call on yours each and every time you're in front of people.

If you find it impossible to assess yourself, see if you can get someone to videotape you speaking at home in a casual, off-handed way, and then during a business activity, preferably a presentation of some sort. If you don't have video capability, audiotape yourself instead. In fact, in some respects that's even better, because I want you to focus on how you *sound*, not how you look.

Play back the tape several times. Become aware of when you're at your best and when you falter. Again, pay close attention to the phrasing and the pauses (what we call beats) in between words and/or sentences. I can assure you that you're in for a weird awakening and, in many instances, probably a very pleasant one. I want you to be proud!

Video and audio taping are wonderful ways to scrutinize your *overall performance*, but this time I want you to monitor your timing only. Once you become acquainted with *your* style, it will become like a repetitive tune in your head — where you start, where you naturally break, the speeding up, the slowing down. You'll soon know when you're hitting all the right notes, so to speak. This task of enhancing your timing is one more element in building your unique style. I don't care how many speakers there are, no one else is YOU!

One way to understand the point I'm making is to carefully listen to the phrasing, musically speaking, of different singers and musicians. Each has his or her own stop and start points, places where they pause, notes they emphasize, etc.

Remember what I said earlier about layering all these so-called "Miller" ingredients. When combined, they produce a more effective you. After this chapter, you should have a much better handle on the nature of timing — what constitutes it, how to detect it, how to recognize your own, and how to put yours to work to your best advantage.

In addition to replaying video and audio tapes of yourself, begin to observe the people around you. If you're a networking type, you probably go to plenty of functions where you can assess your colleagues. If one of your associates happens to be the speaker, see if there's a marked difference in his or her timing in conversation with you before the speech, and then up at the podium while delivering it.

Grab opportunities to listen to an entire group, like when the participants at a breakfast meeting do their 60-second intro bit. Is their timing as superb as it was when they were engaged in casual conversation with you? Do they "lose it" when they stand and deliver? These kinds of observations are terrifically helpful to you in your study of timing. And if you're an ardent student, you'll begin to pick up on all kinds of things that previously would have escaped you.

You may find one or two people, in particular — friends, colleagues, or even professional performers — whose timing really appeals to you. Ask yourself why; then study them independently, on a frequent basis. Take notes when your business associates talk, keeping your attention focused squarely on their timing. Rent videos and study the timing of actors. Listen to your favorite singers and musicians.

One of the last points I want to make about timing is that when it constantly changes — when there are variations in the manner of dialogue delivery, when people are caught off guard and don't know what to expect next, when they're truly surprised — that's when great timing is fully implemented. Anything less is monotony!

In addition to watching your fellow workers and professional performers, I want you to also put the spotlight on yourself. Pick one or more of the *physical* exercises you enjoy regularly that rely on timing — activities such as dancing, dribbling a basketball, swimming, shooting pool, running, aerobics, juggling, etc. Then do one and check out the way you move; check out your rhythm. Next, pick a *mental* activity that demands timing, such as keeping the beat to your favorite music, writing a limerick, playing Nintendo. Remember what you're up to: You want to increase the sharpness of your "ear."

Finally, I want you to do at least one of the following exercises every single day, as a way of guiding you toward better timing. You want timing to become ingrained, subconscious, automatic, rather than something you have to think about consciously. Remember this, too: Good timing is the difference between being a hit or a miss!

1. If you glanced over this chapter, here's a reminder: Listen to sounds, both mechanical and natural. Just listen. In addition, do one physical and one mental activity that relies on timing.

2. Upgrade the sharpness and clarity of your hearing by lis-

tening to sounds that are harder to discern. For example, focus on the background vocals on an Aretha Franklin recording (or the artist of your preference); or the secondary noises made by your washing machine. Now, snap your fingers or tap your toes in *time* with *that* beat.

3. Get someone to write down the first line of a poem. Recite that line out loud and then keep going, making up an entire poem. One easy way to accomplish this is to repeat the first line as if it's the refrain. Keep all your stanzas in *time*, though. Your made-up poem should have a distinctive beat. It's in there somewhere. If you're having difficulty, pick up some liner notes from one of your CDs or tapes and notice how lyrics are written. Read some out loud. Snap your fingers as you go.

4. Speaking of lyrics, here's another exercise I want you to do. Listen to a song with words, the kind where the words don't always rhyme. Carly Simon and Joni Mitchell write this way, as does Kenny Loggins at times. Maybe all of the end words don't rhyme, but the timing of these singers makes it sound as if they do. This is a pretty sophisticated assignment, but a fun one. The works of Jackson Browne, Bob Dylan, and The Eagles are really great for seeing how precisely and tightly lyrics *can* be written. In addition, you can listen to rap music. With that type of music, timing is also very important; and you'll be able to see how well each syllable falls into meter. Please feel free to pick your own favorites in each category as you do this assignment.

5. This one is easy and healthy, too! Dance!!!! Turn on some music and dance IN TIME. You may find that you've been dancing against the beat — i.e., rushing it, bogging down. Stay right on the beat. Listen for drums as a guidepost if you need to. Your assignment is to move to the music with precision.

6. In keeping with the above task, see if you can recruit one or more partners to dance with you. That's right, all of you together, in a circle. Now, one at a time take turns copying the way the other person dances. The one who's being impersonated can dance in the center of the circle. Everyone

else should follow that person's steps, movements, and even attitude. Keep switching until everyone has a turn in the center. This is great discipline for understanding others. When you can feel and get into other people's timing, you tend to have a more accurate impression of where they're coming from. It's kind of like dancing around in the other guy's shoes!

7. Pretend you're a machine. (This may seem bizarre, but all my students are required to do it.) If possible, ask someone you know to throw a suggestion at you or write down a few that you can pick from. Then start with one noise that the machine makes, keeping it constant and regulated. Then add another sound in between, and so on. Try to include as many sounds as you can, keeping them repetitive and exact. Who knows? Maybe you'll be able to accompany Al Jarreau or Bobby McFerrin one day!

    A fun variation on this is to do an "attitude" machine. For example, you can do a smart-aleck machine and make sounds that illustrate that attitude. When you do this, try it in front of a mirror. If you can get a group together, do it as a team. It's a wonderful workout for everyone. I've noticed that children are particularly adept at this one. It's good for training their little ears!

8. Take a specific day and time each week and spend at least one hour just listening to sounds. You might take in a concert, listen to your Walkman, sit on a sailboat listening to the water smack against the underside as the boat rocks, or find a construction crew with a jackhammer. There are no rules for this one. Just do it!

For additional timing exercises you can refer to Chapter 22, "What's So Funny?". It has several that relate closely to this chapter.

"Can you repeat that? Yeah... now I'm listening... go ahead."

Chapter 16

HEAR! HEAR!

The Art of Listening

Here's one for you — true story: This guy named Jerry Walker was talking to another guy, Brad Densworth. Jerry was to introduce Brad, who was that evening's speaker at Jerry's association meeting. I overheard Brad tell Jerry that he had been a motivational speaker in San Diego for ten years; had been a stand-up comic working at the Improv in Brea, California for the last two months; and had received numerous awards, including one for his passion, which was aviation research. Jerry was frantically scribbling all this down on a napkin. He was sorry, he admitted, that he'd lost Brad's bio.

Jerry approached the podium, taking his very large ego with him. He cleared his throat loudly into the microphone as he said, "Ladies and gentlemen...is this thing on? It is? Oh, I didn't hear him say...he did? Anyway, I'm here to introduce tonight's speaker, Brad Densman, a stand-up comic at the Comedy Store, who speaks to motivators and has for over ten years, and" — tossing a cocky smile Brad's way — "oh, yes, Brad's into planes. I guess he flies his own plane. He's even won an award for flying. Brad?"

Brad smiled thinly, trying to hide his displeasure. Pro that he was, he took his place before the group and made what turned out to be a wonderful speech. He began, however, by gently correcting the misinformation that Jerry had passed along. Jerry cringed. I was embarrassed for both of them. Jerry hadn't listened to Brad at all, or perhaps in making the napkin translation, he'd botched the facts considerably. This isn't uncommon; in fact, it happens every day in every boardroom and hotel meeting facility across America. I wish I had a dollar for every misconstrued "fact" for just one day of speaker introductions. Who needs the lottery!

The bottom line with regard to the Jerry/Brad intro fiasco is that everyone involved was penalized. Jerry made a fool of himself; Brad was slightly humiliated; and the audience was the most uncomfortable of all. Talk about setting the wrong tone! And this scenario doesn't apply just to speeches either; it's also played out every day at meetings, one-on-one exchanges, etc. It's rampant, an epidemic.

I stated earlier that the chapter on spontaneity might be the most important "Miller" chapter. Well, let me just say that this one is the *second* most important. Why? In my opinion, listening to others is the area where communicators (including myself) are the most deficient. I would guess that, on average, we *hear* 50 percent of what's said, but actually *listen* to only about 15 percent of that. The trouble is, this one communication shortcoming causes us more problems than any other.

Not only on the job, either.

The reasons for poor listening run the gamut. Some people get distracted only momentarily, while others are intensely preoccupied. There are some who are clearly not present, not "in the moment;" others who only hear what they want to hear; and still others whose minds are simply dry-docked, beached somewhere — disengaged from the rest of their being. However, I think the most common reason for NOT listening is that people are so consumed with themselves that they can't break away long enough to place the emphasis on someone else.

Incidentally, one basic improv fundamental taught in the early stages of training is that each actor is to think only about how he or she can serve and support the other actors in the scene. Actors learn to take the focus off themselves and put it on everyone else. You can only imagine what the results would be if each of us did that during our everyday business activities.

The ability to say nothing and just listen is one of the most powerful selling tools available to us. When we re-use information (a heavily-relied upon utensil in the cooking of the improv player's stew), we impress the hell out of people. What I'm explicitly referring to is the ability to just absorb, to take in and play off *that* information quickly and appropriately. Focusing solely on what comes out of the other guy's mouth, assimilating, and then reacting to it is absolutely the best way I know to make someone else feel special and important. This is a prerequisite to selling; you must give your undivided attention to others. How can you make the impression — or make the sale — without first giving people what they need? And what they need, first and foremost, is for *you* to listen to *them*! Through listening attentively we provide understanding.

Not listening could cost you the sale. Maybe it has. Sure, some of us are great with details as they relate to the product part, but we're not very good at details when it comes to the people part. BECAUSE WE DON'T LISTEN! I'm not referring just to the spoken word either. I'm also talking about the subtext — what is *unsaid*.

Subtext is even more important than the spoken message. It's what lies beneath the surface, what is said silently. Everyone's dialogue comes with a big helping of subtext underneath it.

First, though, let's talk about the spoken word and the problem of superficial listening. How much do you really hear? Do you stay in the moment, or do you get stuck on something you heard three sentences ago and fail to keep up with the speaker? Do you drift in and out of other people's explanations and requests? Are you able to focus only on what seems beneficial or important to you?

Chew on this for a minute: Our minds have a mind of their own! Thoughts are like rebellious teenagers; they tend to come and go — oftentimes without warning. On the whole, we as a species are innately undisciplined when it comes to listening intently, to receiving spoken messages in their entirety during every step of our conversations. It's just not natural for us. The good news is that we can work at it; we can increase our ability to listen attentively to others.

Earlier, I listed some causes for poor listening. I want to add one other: boredom. If you're captivated by the other person(s), you stay tuned in. If you're not, you don't. You might want to take note of how many conversations are difficult to listen to mainly because they're boring! I know that boredom causes problems for me. But I don't have the luxury of listening selectively, or of listening only when I feel like it. None of us does, really. Our job — every one of us — is to *really* listen to the people who are talking to us. If we want to be good communicators, we simply must discipline ourselves to also be good listeners.

I can't tell you how many times I've been at a presentation or speech where the audience interacted with the speaker, but the speaker didn't really listen to what someone in the audience was asking. Instead, he or she responded from a personal vantage point or missed the mark altogether. No wonder relationships fail!

Now, in the world of the improv player, the failure to listen can mean sudden death! Each player must rely on the dialogue of the other players. A scene can't progress unless each response is threaded sequentially with what preceded it. So if the players aren't *constantly* listening, that thread is threatened or broken, and the integrity of the scene crashes. At that point, the communication comes to a screeching halt. How many times has the communication in your real-life scenes come to a complete stop?

Remember, too, that improv actors must respond quickly. They don't have time to sit and mull over a thought, nor do they have the freedom to listen only to what appeals to them. So in the course of their training, their listening acumen is whipped into shape. As a result, their "ear" becomes razor sharp; and the quicker the ear has to move, the more finely tuned the listening muscle becomes.

Here's another interesting aspect of the improv credo: Improv players are required to respond to the very last thing that is said. Always. If an improv player wants to contribute during a scene, he or she must "add information" to the last thing that was said or the last idea held. Then the next player adds something to that, and so on and so on and so on. It's one of the tricks that makes a completely improvised scene play as if it's been written beforehand. Without keen listening skills, however, the improv players would hit and miss — be in and out of their communication on stage. I, and the other improv players I know, put very heavy emphasis on this aspect of fundamental improv instruction.

As a speaker, presenter, and communicator, you're no different than the improv player. If you're not a good listener, you don't get to be a good performer. And once again, we're *all* performers. If you're not listening to your audience, you can't give them what *they* need. If you can't give them what they need, you won't get what *you* want. It's the proverbial vicious circle; it just keeps going round and round. The only way you can break out of such a cycle is to develop a sharper ear.

Let's address listening with regard to subtext (what's unsaid). This is not as easy as listening superficially, of course, but it is the key to listening fully. Someone can say, "Oh, I'm having a great day;" and depending on the person's tone, facial expression, body language, and nuance, those few words may say something entirely different from the literal translation.

I can't think of a single instance when I've listened to someone — speaker or not — who didn't have a modicum of subtext going on. Gearing our responses to the subtext is what makes us brilliant communicators (and salespeople). To be able to deal with subtext, though, we must allow ourselves to make use of two other mental muscles: instinct and perception. Although instinct and perception may seem more like feeling muscles than thinking muscles, the functions of both are used in improv. Feeling and thinking functions are interrelated in every scene, every improv game, and every improv piece of work. We each have those gifts readily available to us, if we care to use them.

In real life, I think people have a tendency to listen to what is said and to play off that, rather than taking the subtext into consideration and demonstrating understanding by relaying that back. For example, if someone said to me, "Oh, I'm having a great day," but there was sarcasm in her voice, she rolled her eyes slightly, her shoulders heaved a bit, and she sighed heavily, I wouldn't say, "Oh, that's nice; so am I." Rather, I would attend to the real message. Perhaps I would say, "Sorry. Is there anything I can do?", or "I've had those kinds of days before," or "Tomorrow is another day," or maybe, "Tell me about it." With any of those responses, I would have instantly connected, bonded, or — in the words of John Lennon and Paul McCartney — "come together" with that person. Without verbalizing it, she would know that I was *truly* listening to what she had to say. Incidentally, in the process I would have established rapport.

Now, granted, the example I've given is a fairly simple one; but these types of communications occur every day to each of us. Often we skate right by them without a flicker of understanding. The truth is, we're not listening.

In dealing with people, I've trained myself to listen to subtext first, and then the actual words. In presentations, during speeches, when I'm part of a panel, I know I have to be agile enough to respond to the needs of the person asking the question. Depending on what my listening tells me, I may change my style, my approach, my parlance. My first priority is to connect, and I know that's one way to do it.

Listening to subtext produces tight communication. Tight communication equals understanding, and that's what our "buyers" want. Detecting subtext is a skill that we should all use during every communication encounter.

So I think we can agree that we all need to work on becoming better listeners. The guidelines for effective listening are simple: focus; concentrate; stay in the moment. As you're listening to someone speak, notice whether you're doing these three things. If not, get back on track! Remember, if you're not doing all three, you're *not* really listening.

Following are exercises to help you improve your listening skills. Some exercises you can do alone, but most of the listening exercises I'm going to assign require one or more persons. These ExecuProv workouts are fun, so finding others to join in should be easy.

Here are some exercises you can do alone:

1. Listen to a news report or something on radio or television. Just for a minute or two. Record it if you have the technical capability. Now see if you can repeat it back. Play back the recording to see how accurate your recitation was.

2. Listen to someone with an interesting dialect or affectation and see if you can impersonate that person. Or watch someone, and see if you can imitate his or her walk, laugh, or

gestures (this falls more into the subtext mode). It's great fun and should also provide a little nudge toward lessening your inhibitions.

3. If you have children, really listen to them — to *everything* they say. You'll probably be astounded. (Most of the time we're such abusive listeners when it comes to our children. We do a lot of "uh-huh..." Especially with the little ones, or those that seem to chatter away.) Then see if you can repeat back what they said. Also, check out their subtexts.

4. As you sit in a meeting or at a speech, listen to who's talking, but before the person begins, pick a simple word like "the," and every time that word is used, keep score by marking it on a notepad, tapping your toe, scratching your ear — anything that will indicate to you that you've heard the pre-assigned word. Although you'll be listening for a particular word, you'll be paying attention to the rest of the dialogue as well.

5. The next time you're on the phone or meeting with someone, take copious notes. Your notes should include what was said and what wasn't. Reviewing the notes afterward could be very enlightening. If you're a salesperson, the next time you make a sales call, either in person or on the phone, take notes. This has a way of making other people feel good, because you're demonstrating that their words — which express their needs and ideas — are very important to you. This is a positive way of monitoring your listening, and saying "I care."

6. Along the same lines as above: Take minutes at your next meeting. You have to keep up with what's being said every second so that your notes will be complete and accurate. This is a tough one, but I'd like you to do it at least once a week. Pretend that you're doing a "Dear Diary" thing, and write down everything that you hear — in the words and also in the subtext.

7. Select one person for the day — let's say a co-worker — and see if you can make a list of the most important things the person said during a half or full day. Keep jotting down

things. Review your notes later that day or the next. You might have an awakening experience. I did this with my youngest son not along ago, and it was a mind blower!

8. If you get the chance to overhear a conversation, do so (without invading privacy, of course). It's always intriguing to listen in while others converse. Sitting on the sidelines makes for a great study. I suggest this exercise because we all seem interested in other people's conversations. Pay close attention to subtext here. Is there irritation? Hostility? Maybe someone's flirting!

9. When someone speaks — and if you're not taking notes — look at the person. In improv we call this "attending to." It causes you to pay attention and to *listen* more intently. How many times do you look at the person who's talking to you? It's a must in an improv scene. Each player is required to be looking at whoever's speaking, most of the time. This ensures keener listening!

The following are exercises for you and a partner or partners:

1. As a regular drill: Sit face-to-face with someone and have that person tell you his or her life story in 1-2 minutes. Ask the person to use lots of names, dates, places, etc. When the person is finished, repeat the information back as accurately as possible. Don't drift; stay with the person through every sentence.

2. This exercise also requires another person — the more, the merrier. I like to see this game used during staff meetings as a warm-up. As you converse, each person must begin his or her sentence with the last letter of the last word that was just spoken. For instance, if someone says, "I want another cup of coffee," a correct response would be something like "Everybody wants another cup." The next person would then say, "Perhaps you're right." This is really fun and forces every participant to stay 100 percent tuned in.

3. Ask your partner to think of a famous cliche, like "Blood is thicker than water," "Nothing ventured, nothing gained," "Hang in there," etc. Instead of telling you what the cliche is, your partner should carry on a one-sided dialogue that

discusses the essence of what the cliche means, without using any words that are included in it. See if you can guess what the cliche is. Now, this takes cooperation from both of you, because you have to play to each other's way of conveying information. It's a great lesson in perception on both sides.

4. This exercise takes friends, co-workers, or family. Sit in a circle, and have the person say, "I saw a brown dog." The second person has to repeat that sentence and add something to it — for instance, "I saw a brown dog, and a gray mustache." The next person may say, "I saw a brown dog, a gray mustache, and a flying Volkswagen." Keep building on the phrases, and keep going around the circle as many times as you can. This can be done with two people or ten. This is a wonderful focus and concentration exercise, and also helps with memory retention.

Closing notes:

1. Challenge yourself on a daily basis to write down something you've heard before, but initially didn't *really* hear at all. It could be as simple as church chimes down the street. Keep listening for new things.

2. Pause each day and quiet yourself for five minutes. Close your eyes. Just listen to the sounds around you. What do you hear? If there is silence, listen to how that sounds. I guarantee that you'll hear something you haven't noticed before.

"Oh, dear! Body language, what **did** they say about body language?
Wonder if I can keep one hand up here, one in there, my legs crossed…???"

Chapter 17

You Don't Have to Say It — Your Body Just Did

Body Language and What It Says For You

I don't claim to be an expert in body language, but as a speech coach, I do know what does — and doesn't — play well in terms of body movements. My credentials come from my work as a director of live theater, particularly sketch work, musical comedy, and improvisational comedy.

You see, while directors are trained to monitor the actors' performances with regard to things like dialogue, scene content, and flow, they're also required to create and nurture what is called "stage picture." Let me explain. In improv there is very little, if any, furniture or other props. Just the same, the audience has to get a very specific picture of what the actors are dealing with in terms of "things," both real and inanimate. Examples might include a subway strap, refrigerator door, steering wheel, dog, child, or bartender. These visuals must be created from the imaginations of the actors, and then communicated to the audience in a way that enables them to share in the mental picture.

That being the case, the director must have a very keen eye, always making sure that there is congruency from moment to moment, and that all physical movements are consistent and appropriate. After a time, the director develops almost a built-in alarm that is triggered whenever an actor is out of sync with what's appropriate in terms of his or her body language.

133

Here's something else: At times actors both move and talk; at other times they only move. (As a matter of fact, they pantomime a lot.) Those body movements — or body language — have to send very strong and deliberate signals to the other actors and the audience. There is one improv learning exercise where the actors are required to begin the scene with 30 seconds of silence. In that 30 seconds they have to set the tone of the scene and establish their relationship to one another and the activity that is taking place, *before* they're allowed to utter even one word of dialogue. This exercise demonstrates to students the importance and power of physical movement, which is also the reason that we directors often require our students to pantomime entire pieces of work.

I make sure that my ExecuProv students do these same exercises, in order to increase their awareness of the importance of body language. So the root, then, of the "Miller" theory of body language comes from my work as a director of live theater, especially improv comedy.

One thing I truly dislike — but which I see a lot of — is the stand-'em-up/line-'em-up improv scene. That's when the actors are positioned in almost a straight line across the stage, and they just stand there and exchange dialogue throughout the scene. In your vernacular, it's commonly referred to as the "talking heads" deal; and that's exactly the point I want to make. As an actor or a speaker, it's easy to get trapped in a constricted format.

Why does this happen? I think it's because performers and speakers are so focused on their verbal presentation, they forget that they must create a visual presentation as well. In addition, people spend a lot of time sitting at their desks, delivering dialogue over the phone, and also in meetings, where they talk while remaining glued to the chair. Just because you have limited space, though, doesn't mean that you must forego action. Granted, it should always be action that is appropriate to the situation; for example, you can't be sitting at a meeting and use the same gestures that you'd use at the podium before a crowd of 250 people. But you can enhance your "moment" with physicality. Just be sure to make adjustments: the smaller the space, the more subtle the movement. Movement, though — what a powerful tool!

From the back of the room, I once saw a guy at the podium, and the only thing that moved on his whole being was his mouth. Mostly his bottom lip. The rest of him looked like one of those wax figures at the Movieland Wax Museum in Buena Park, Ca.; you could swear they're real, but no go. (I confess that I once visited that facility and impulsively blurted out something to JFK, something like "Who really did it, Jack?" Naturally, no response. The people with me dispersed in bullet-like fashion, scrambling in several directions so the other visitors wouldn't think we were together.)

Well, if you're the type who just stands at the podium like a statue, guess what? First off, you're boring. And second, there's no human connection! Remember what I said earlier: Your job is to entertain your audience. You do that not just with content, but also with movement.

YOU must create a strong visual to keep your audience interested and focused on you. If the only thing the audience really wanted to do was *listen* to you, they could buy your audiotape or call you on the phone. But in a live speech or presentation setting, the audience is there to see you IN ACTION. So it's incumbent upon you to give them a great show. An important part of that show is "stage picture."

Earlier in "Miller," I mentioned that you have two primary assets with which to communicate: your voice and your face. To some extent, though, you also have your body; so think of it this way: Your most important communication tools are your voice and your face, with body language being secondary. But it's still very important to use it appropriately in order to express yourself fully.

There are no precise guidelines for how and when to use body language. It should be somewhat instinctive. In other words, if you're in sync with yourself — if you're delivering dialogue with ease, energy, and spontaneity, and truly being yourself — the body language that accompanies your vocal and facial expressions will probably fall into place naturally, without effort or thought. Remember how you are with your best friend in the kitchen: You don't force your head, arms, hands, and shoulders to move in a particular way; they just do their thing. Well, the same principle applies on the job.

I truly dislike watching speakers, presenters or meeting leaders whose movements seem contrived and deliberate. The audience shouldn't be conscious of your movements; instead, those movements should simply serve to punctuate your presence by creating an interesting visual that adds some activity to your presentation. However, if viewers are too conscious of your actions, it means that you're forcing the movements, overdoing them, using them at inappropriate times, or displaying nervous tics. To overcome this problem, you'll need to adjust the tracking on your "stage picture."

I hope this doesn't sound mean, but as a stage director, I seem almost magnetically drawn to evidence of even the slightest nervous tic in a speaker. There my attention stays glued, as I chuckle silently to myself. And believe me, I've seen everything.

Here are some common ones from guys. They pull relentlessly on the knot of their tie, rock toe to heel, reach continually into their left breast suit pocket (what's in there anyway?), run their fingers down the chord muscles of their neck, or offer a half-cocked grin while pointing in the opposite direction from their overhead or visual aid. My all-time favorite, though — and you see this when guys are standing podium-less, waiting for their introductions to be completed — is when they cup their hands proudly in front of their crotch and steal a quick ball scratch, thinking that we won't notice.

Now, here are some I've witnessed when women are in the spotlight. They adjust their Wonder Bra with the inside of their bicep, rock from side to side wearing a coquettish grin on their flushed faces, clear away the lipstick build-up in their lip corners, continually push the nose grip of their eyeglasses upward (sometimes I swear that they're going to shove those glasses right through their forehead), stand with one hip thrust forward, or slip their heels in and out of their pumps. My favorite among the female species is when they toss their hair back over a shoulder or two. (I once saw someone do this so frantically that her hair got wrapped around her necklace, and she nearly choked to death.) Also on the subject of hair, there are those women who tuck their tresses so firmly behind their ears as they go along that by the end of the speech, they've often created an entirely different hairdo — unintentionally, of course.

As an aside, I just want to mention that most of the weird body language we display when under pressure can be traced to our younger years, from childhood. For instance, when women are nervous, I often see them turn slightly from side to side as they speak, heads cocked sideways and down a bit, eyes looking upward, with hands clasped and fingers pulling on one another. This is the same body language they used as young girls when they sought approval, asking Daddy if he liked their new dress, or when giving that first book report in second grade, where all the sentences ran together. Some women carry with them into adulthood an exact replica of that early body expression, while for others, traces of it may appear only when they have to stand up before that all-important group.

In the case of men, one of the most prevalent, left-over-from-childhood expressions of body language is where they cock the head back just a bit, thrust up the shoulders, and then rock toe to heel. This is high school or college macho stuff that says something like "Hey, I just got a D in history, but who cares, I'm still cool." I'll never forget Mike Smith, sales rep for a printing company, who was receiving an award for his work. They called his name, he popped out of his chair, and ran toward the podium exactly the way football players run onto the field in front of the TV cameras when their names are called on game day. You know the drill. They do a lateral run, abruptly turn front and center, smile, and then take off. Well, the only thing missing from Mike Smith the night I saw him was his football uniform. As he accepted his trophy, he even nuzzled it under his right armpit the same way a football player would cradle his helmet. (To this day, I wonder if his chest was really that broad, or was he never quite able to let go of his shoulder pads!)

Believe it or not, these are just a few of the examples of inappropriate body language I've witnessed. There have been many others. In fact, there is one other that's worth mentioning, because, for me, it really took the cake — my all-time favorite in the category of "worsts": the butt scratcher. (And hey, without a podium, that's hell to watch for 45 minutes!)

Now we've talked about both the absence of body language and how detrimental that can be, and also about how people can overuse their bodies or use movements that send the wrong message, which can be equally harmful to a speech or presentation. So perhaps you'll want to have someone videotape your next speech or presentation to find out if you have any age-inappropriate body language working against you, or any body language going on that you're unaware of and might be better off without. (Remember the butt scratcher!)

The truth is, when we're under stress, we regress, or revert to familiar patterns, without being conscious of doing so. That's when we're most likely to display nervous tics, too. So while our words may be eloquent, our bodies may be sending messages that are entirely contradictory. For example, if you say, "I'm feeling very proud to be here today," but you look down at the floor — even for a fleeting second — while delivering those words, you've just sent an unconscious message to the audience that you're not sure of yourself.

I've read that 93 percent of our message is conveyed nonverbally, so — and please pardon this pun if it applies to you — your body carries a lot of weight! In addition, it's said that approximately 88 percent of what we say and do is picked up by the receiver's unconscious mind. Again, pretty powerful stuff. If you can remember that your body language conveys to the audience a picture of what's going on inside you, this will help you stay centered and conscious of your movements. Don't forget, though, that while sometimes these movements are overt and obvious, it's more common for them to be very subtle. And speaking of common, the most negative messages of all are the ones that say, "I'm not worthy," "I have no confidence," or "I feel inadequate." So remember, don't look down when you're speaking.

Like great actors, you always want to perform with aplomb, no matter what you're feeling on the inside.

As I stated earlier, I'm not an expert in body language, but I do know what works from a director's eye. When it comes to body expression, I coach each of my ExecuProv students differently, because everyone is unique unto himself (or herself) in terms of how they use their bodies. I want my students to be able to maximize and integrate all of their communication resources — mental, verbal, and physical. It's the *combination* of these resources that produces truly powerful communicators.

The following should provide some simple guidelines and help put you in touch with what your body is saying:

1. Try to keep both hands visible during a presentation, whether it takes place at a podium or a meeting table. At the unconscious level, a sense of distrust is felt by your viewers when one or both of your hands disappear from sight (i.e., they may be wondering, unconsciously, what you're doing with the other hand or hands). Hands also can be used to symbolize openness, and with an outward, open-palmed gesture, you can welcome your audience. As you pull the palm back toward you, you invite people in. Never put your hands in your pockets, behind your back, or worst of all, let them dangle awkwardly at your sides. Remember, your hands are supposed to be used to make appropriate gestures and movements according to your dialogue. When they're not in use, they need to be in a visible resting position. ALWAYS LET YOUR HANDS FOLLOW YOUR DIALOGUE NATURALLY!

2. When speaking or presenting, always keep your hands at waist height or above. As a performer, you want your audience to focus on your face and upper body. They *should not be aware of your lower body*, unless you're using it to demonstrate something. (It's as if your audience is a camera, and they're zooming in.) *Always* keep your hands at waist height or above. It looks more sophisticated to have your hands there, more dignified. Remember, the eye will tend to go where the hands go; so if your hands are resting against your sides or crotch, that's where your audience will be looking. Instead, you want your energy concentrated; you want your audience focused mainly on your face, and secondarily on your upper body. You won't need to be using your hands at all times, so a good resting position is to hold them gently clasped together at the waistline. You can also allow them to remain there unclasped as well. *It feels weird, but it looks great.* This positioning of the hands gives you a more conservative, executive look; but if your dialogue is conversational and natural, the combination of the dialogue and the

hand positioning says, "I'm in charge, but I'm also human and approachable."

3. If your lower body is constantly in motion, you'll distract your audience, and the message you send will be anything but professional. Moving the lower part of your body while speaking is one of the most embarrassing things you can do to yourself. Professional performers have so much grace, but they rarely use their lower bodies. Watch them and take note.

4. With regard to the above, attend a live theater performance and observe how actors move about the stage. Pay close attention to how they use their bodies. You'll notice that most of their movement — and consequently, your focus — is confined to their faces. You're scarcely aware that they have bodies below the waist, because they're too busy animating their faces, punching their voices, and sending signals with their hands, arms, shoulders, and upper torso.

5. Don't look down. It sends a very strong message that you're feeling inadequate, inferior, insecure. Keep your head at chin level or above. Play up and out. This may sound odd, but if you have a dog, notice how easy it is to tell how the animal feels about itself by the head position alone. If they're in trouble or being reprimanded, they look downward, bowing their heads; if they're frightened, they walk forward in that position. If they're happy or proud, they walk with their heads held extremely level and high. This exercise may sound stupid, but hey, as far as I'm concerned, you're an actor now, so you'll find yourself needing to study all kinds of weird things.

6. In keeping with the above advice, watch the Academy Awards or some similar show where performers are followed by the camera as they take the podium. Most of them will walk with shoulders back and heads at chin level. They seem to glide across the stage. They look so "celebrity," as one student once told me, but fame has nothing to do with it. They carry themselves well; that's all. They've been trained to walk and carry themselves in a certain way. You, too, can have the same look and finesse. Stand straight, take even, but firm and light-footed steps, and look straight ahead. Look

down only for safety reasons, such as a step or obstacle in your path. Otherwise, there's no reason to look at the floor. One word about footsteps, even on a carpeted floor: Don't pound your way across the stage. On the wooden floor of a real theatrical stage, actors learn to walk softly. If you'll notice, you never hear their feet, unless it's for effect.

7. If you have a tendency to look downward while collecting your thoughts, reverse that gesture by looking upward instead, or toward the back corner of the ceiling. It plays so much better; you'll look much more sure of yourself as you ponder what to say. I know I'm repeating myself, but once again, never, ever, ever look down!

8. Keep your lower body still and planted. Make sure that your legs are slightly apart to help with balance. Lock your knees if you have to in order to feel steady and solid. Now, use your upper body to animate with; let it speak for you.

9. Cross the stage only when it's necessary or there's a reason to do so. Moving too much or too briskly about the stage drives the audience nuts. When I teach stage presence, I tell my students to walk, plant, and then deliver. It keeps them from walking around too much, and makes them aware of the amount of their movement, so they'll know whether to add or subtract to it.

10. Never turn your back to the audience while you're speaking, or even when you're not speaking. Try to walk backward to that map, visual, graph, etc., and keep talking as you continue to face the audience. Every time you turn your back on them, you temporarily break the connection. Actors rarely turn their backs to the audience, unless it's part of the blocking direction — which, incidentally, is done only to make a specific point. If actors do turn their backs to the audience, they're usually not delivering dialogue at the same time. There is a term used in theater called "playing to the fourth wall." If the areas beside and behind you are considered the first, second, and third walls, then the audience is the fourth wall. As a performer, that's where your focus should always be. Play to that fourth wall, unless people are seated alongside you; then you must play to them also.

11. If you're seated on a panel or there are others "on stage" with you, make sure you're not blocking them and they're not upstaging you in some way. The audience should be able to view all the "players;" otherwise, they can become frustrated and annoyed. Also, if you're seated in a peculiar place and have your back half-turned to the audience, which happens often on the dais, cheat out. In other words, turn forward a bit or to a three-quarter position so that the audience can get a good view of you.

12. Try to keep your hands off your face. Actors are taught not to scratch their noses during a performance, whether it's live or in front of a camera. It looks really tacky. Do you touch your face a lot when speaking? Check it out!

13. Begin to notice how many motions of your head, neck, shoulders, arms, and hands can be magical and captivating. Don't overuse physical gestures, but do use them. Experiment with your many different moves and looks. Remember that you need to create "stage picture," and you can't do that if you're doing the statue thing. One fun exercise begins with you standing in front of the mirror. Don't speak; just give yourself an attitude adjustment like, let's say, proud. Then see if your body language can reflect that attitude in the way you hold yourself and the way you move.

14. At the risk of sounding like your mother, sit up straight. There's nothing worse than a sloucher, whether walking or sitting. Poor posture says "I feel bad about myself." This is especially important as you sit on the dais and in meetings. If you're calling on clients, they'll instantly notice your posture — on an unconscious level at the very least.

15. Make certain you pay attention to facial animation when you're considering body language. Your facial expressions, including the use of your features and facial muscles, constitute very strong body language signals. Incidentally, smiling is a very effective signal for you to be broadcasting.

16. Body language communicates power, strength, and self-assurance; it can also translate into being seductive, alluring, and enticing. For this reason, I want you to watch some

movies featuring your favorite actors and study their movements. Turn off the volume; it will make it easier for you to focus on their body language. You did something similar with your facial animation homework, but in this case you're more interested in upper torso movement and gestures.

17. Keep your movements appropriate to the venue you're playing. Obviously, you won't play your movements big if you're seated at a small meeting table — learn to pull it in then. But when the room is big and the audience is large, you'll have to play your gestures grander. Learn to intuitively gauge what is appropriate to the environment, the occasion, and the audience.

"Who's got something to say before I get started?"

Chapter 18

WHO ARE THOSE GUYS, ANYWAY?

Smelling Your Audience

I know business professionals who are very proud of their ability to prepare for a speech, presentation, workshop or pitch. They've gone to great lengths to gather all the facts and figures, graphs and overheads, quotes and analogies. That's nice. But many of these same people don't have a clue as to who their audiences are, or a sense of where their audiences are coming from.

I'm not suggesting that all business professionals are ignorant about the groups they're talking to. However, their knowledge often consists of generalizations, such as the "Marketing Guys," the "Management Team," the "Chamber," the "Administrative Staff," and so on.

For a moment at least, let's give you and other business professionals the benefit of the doubt and say that you know who comprises your audiences. As an example, let's say that you're a tax attorney who's about to speak before 23 CPAs from southern California. The audience is there to learn about the newest legislation relative to tax law. Terrific. That much you know. Of course, you're there because you're the expert in the field. But — and it's a big "but" — to heck with you for a minute, because your presence there is secondary. The audience is primary. And guess what? *Every audience is different.* And that's the problem: We don't play to each audience differently. Instead, we just roll along with our pre-planned agenda and give it to 'em the same ol' way, each time, every time. Often, we hardly even consider the audience. We just know that they're there, like they're supposed to be. That's why *we're* there!

When you study the mechanics of what makes a good improv show work, you come to the realization that the audience is the first priority. Sorry about pounding you over the head with improv fundamentals again, but this is just one more reason why improv comedy training is so very valuable. See, improv actors never play to every audience the same way. Instead, we learn to vary our scenes and dialogue based on the "temperature" of the room we're playing. As you've probably guessed, I'm not talking here about temperature as degrees of Fahrenheit or Celsius! I'm talking about the prevailing mood of the group in attendance.

To a large extent, the audience will actually dictate the direction and flavor of our night's work, so our first assignment is always to assess that audience, to get a feel for where they're coming from. We don't actually have the benefit of interviewing them and getting to know them before the show starts, but we do find ways to do what we call "smelling" the audience — which means we tune in and pick up on the general energy in the room.

I know in an earlier chapter I mentioned that audience reaction tends to vary depending on the climate of the people present. Some audiences are loudly responsive, while others are not. It doesn't mean that one group likes the show and the other doesn't. It just means that some people are more vocal with their appreciation than others. Also, some parts of the show seem to resonate with the audience while others do not. Some people laugh at particular lines, but not at others. The following week the exact same show can get a different response to those same lines. Why is that? Different strokes...but I think it's also because every "house" tends to gather, collect, and unconsciously form one general energy field. The mood or level of that field tends to govern the audience's attitude, and thus the nature of their responses for the evening. For example, we've had rowdy audience members, and somehow just a handful of them can stimulate the same mental state in the other guests. The rowdiness tends to give others permission to be more carefree and participatory. On the other hand, we've had audiences that tended to be a bit shy, and this inhibited some of the usually outgoing types, causing them to stay a little quiet.

At the beginning of our shows, I'm always introduced to the audience; and I take the stage to greet them. Presumably they think I'm there to get input for the show, and that's partially true. But what's more important for me is to get a feel for the people we're performing for, so we can cater to their sense of fun. As I ask for suggestions, I banter with members of the audience, always in a playful way, always encouraging them to participate and speak up. This allows me to grab hold of that energy and know exactly where we need to be with that evening's performance. I can usually tell if the actors need to punch their performance with additional energy to get the room "up" more, if they need to soften their punch, or slow down their pace for easier assimilation by audience members. Some audiences are slow to warm up to the show, while others are laughing heartily from the very first scene.

From my first encounter with the audience, I know exactly how the night will go, because we start by always playing off of them. Unconsciously, the audience tells us what they want and need in order to have a good time. I'm not sure how you acquire this ability to "smell" an audience. It isn't something you can just read about and do. I believe it comes with time and experience; it evolves. And you have to rely on your instincts and trust them.

As you already know, I also speak to many groups about the "Miller" theories. Those audiences are always diverse. I'll bet I speak to ten service groups or organizations each month, and each one of those audiences is different in some way. Consequently, each of my presentations is different, too. It's not that I have to eliminate any of my messages and materials; rather, I just shape and mold my presentation according to what the room dictates. If I could create an analogy or metaphor to describe this, I guess I'd say that every time I take the podium, I do this mental "Gumby" thing — I bend and tweak whichever way I need to.

Getting back to my original point: When most business professionals speak, they're so concerned about content and performance that they forget to check out the audience. Some speakers have told me that they don't even remember an audience being there; it's all a blur. They just know people were there. As you already know, the emphasis with "Miller" is on making the human connection; and such a connection is virtually impossible unless you first familiarize yourself with the energy that pervades the room.

I advocate an icebreaker at every event — be it a speech, workshop, sales pitch — because it will give you an instant feel for the people you're trying to sell to. (Don't forget, we're all selling something.) An icebreaker is my first order of business. I then leave myself enough mental room to play to *that* particular audience — to give them the message in a way that I think they'll best be able to receive it, rather than doing the same ol' been there, done that kind of thing.

Preparing the content of your presentation is only one aspect of your job. Working on your style and delivery is another. Still another — and the one I think may be the most important when you break it all down — is the task of "smelling" your audience. It may take some time to master this, but it can be done; and it should be done if you want to make the most of your speaking opportunity. After all, isn't that why you're there? Your audience should always be more important to you than you. For those of you with the really big egos, I know that's a tall order!

The following are a few ways of learning to "smell" your audience, as well as some ideas on how to increase your sensitivity to others:

1. For openers, practice your awareness and concentration exercises; they tend to sharpen your sensitivity on both the obvious and subtextual levels. After a while, you'll come to rely on instincts; you'll be able to feel the audience in a vibration sort of way. And incidentally, this applies whether the audience is one person or 100.

2. Here's another one of those times to let your mind lead you. If you're sitting on a dais or greeting attendees at the door, just absorb the energy. What impressions do you get? Now, play off that, instead of a preconceived notion of how you thought they'd be.

3. As you begin your talk, whatever it is, try an icebreaker. This can be in the form of a joke, a fun story, asking the audience as a group one or more questions, kidding with a certain someone in the audience — the possibilities are endless. The trick? Be as spontaneous as you can be. Don't be so prepared that you can't "go with" the room when you first "take" it. Having a few one-liners that you can depend on to elicit an initial response from the audience is okay, but I'm not a big fan of that. I'd rather you free-wheeled it. That's real bonding stuff. It gives you great confidence, too.

4. Before that presentation, do as much research on the audience as you can, including the company they work for if it's a group from one place. If the audience is a mixed group of people coming from different places, find out what attracted them to your speech or workshop. Most of your presentations, however, will be to already made-up groups like the Chamber of Commerce or the "Marketing Guys" at such and such a company. Background information should be easy to access. Find a point person who can tell you about the group, and about any unusual or interesting people who might be attending your speech or pitch — including their primary interests and concerns, and previous speakers that they might have liked.

5. Watch for body language and eye contact. You can tell a lot about people's moods from those two things alone. Again, use those barometers to determine where to go with your presentation and what attitudes to make use of in your delivery.

6. This you can do on occasion: Try to target the more upbeat, fun-looking, or interested people in the group. Play with them for a moment using some type of verbal exchange. It can change the climate of the rest of the room, set the tone, or shift the energy field at any time. Remember, you want to reach out and grab your audience from the get-go, so I want you to do all you can to establish that mood up front.

7. As you first introduce yourself, do your icebreaker and then give the room over to the audience for a moment; that is, get as many of them as possible responding and chatting with

you. Lay out (that's an improv term for "hold back"), and let them go at it for a minute. Your observation of that exchange should provide you with a strong "sniff" as to where the audience is coming from.

8. After you've learned to "smell" your audience, try to match the audience's energy, or get them to match yours. Don't ever overwhelm them; you'll just turn them off. And don't play "under" them — that is, allow them to intimidate you. If they get a little playful, you get a little playful. If they're shy at first, go at them a little more softly and gently initially. If body language or other indicators are telling you that your audience is tired or bored (this often happens at all-day seminars when audiences go from speech to speech), work at changing their energy — at getting it up. It's called warming up the audience; and that's essentially what I'm doing for my actors when I open the show by talking to the audience for a few minutes.

9. Know your own limits. Don't overdo the getting-to-know-you thing. The audience will be on to you and your pretense; they'll be uncomfortable, and so will you. Then the overall energy in the room will be restless, and the chemistry between you and your audience will gradually disintegrate.

10. Study improv players and stand-up comics. Watch how they interact with their audiences every step of the way. They are continually conscious of what the audience wants and needs, and they give it to them. Ah, yes, the stand-up comic — the perfect example to study.

11. Last note: A great performer will first and foremost "smell" an audience. That enables the performer to connect with the audience, to play *to* and *off* them. Ultimately, that creates a great atmosphere, which increases the opportunities for making the sale. That sale could be in the form of a product or something as simple as getting a laugh. Remember, take the focus off you and your thing, and put it on your audience and their thing. You can't lose that way, and people will find you personable, inviting, and highly connectable. There is something to be said for people who just pick up our vibes, and know just what to say and how to say it.

"Actually, it's really me, Comstock. Is that you in there?"

Chapter 19

WHAT A CHARACTER!

Hiding Behind Yourself or Somebody Else to Bring Out Your Best

I know some of you have the idea that actors have a kind of bravado — an ability to just get up in front of a live audience or go before a camera and feel totally comfortable. For some, that's true; in fact, many actors consider such experiences the ultimate high. But for others — and there are many of them — that's simply not the case. They experience the same physical and mental anxieties that you and I do. For example, I'm told that Steve Martin is very self-effacing; and Carly Simon is reported to have turned down many live concerts and touring dates because she just can't bear the thought of getting up in front of all those people.

I recall seeing the great singer/songwriter Michael Franks at a nightclub once, his sailor hat pulled halfway down his face while he sang. This was during the early days of his career, and it was quite obvious that he would have preferred to be singing in the shower instead. Another time, I had a conversation with the actor Gene Wilder, who was so uptight and uncomfortable that he kept staring at his shoes as he answered my questions in a quiet whisper; he couldn't make any eye contact at all. Laraine Newman, one of my contemporaries at the L.A. Groundlings and a very special friend, wouldn't perform at a Groundlings fund-raising anniversary show on one occasion because she couldn't stand the pressure of a live room. As we sat huddled in my dressing room laughing over old times, she confessed that she had burned out from her work on *Saturday Night Live*. She wasn't going out there, she said, unless it was as a member of the audience.

I've mentioned just a few celebrities. Believe me, there are hundreds more who feel exactly the same way, who feel as uncomfortable and self-conscious as you do at having to perform in front of others.

So, then, how do they do it? How do they manage to give award-winning performances and convince the audience that they have no fear? Well, the answer is: They hide. No, not in a physical sense. They hide behind their characters. They figuratively leave themselves behind and become someone else. Even when these individuals are asked to be themselves and stand up to talk during a political event or an awards ceremony, they still hide. They utilize what we at ExecuProv call "tricks and secrets;" that is, they find ways to actually separate themselves from themselves to function at their best.

I prescribe a collection of such "tricks and secrets" for almost every student I coach. I call it "playing Mr. Potato Head," and it consists of mixing and matching an assortment of traits that allow my clients to be their best. For example, if they're too quiet, I might ask them to pretend that everyone in the audience is hard of hearing, which forces my clients to throw their voices. Or I might tell them that their audience can only read lips, so they'll have to really move their mouths around their words very deliberately to make themselves understood by the audience. This "trick" can easily correct a diction problem.

For those who are completely thrown by the idea that an audience is present, I might ask them to imagine that they're simply in the family room with their significant other or best friend having a comfortable chat, and that everyone in the room is their best friend. Other clients are told to pretend that they're walking like either Clint Eastwood or Gene Hackman, as a way of punching up their presence and power.

I have one student who copes by imagining that he has crazy glue on the bottom of his shoes. This helps him to stay planted and prevents him from walking back and forth too much. Another student likes to think of the back of his chair as Sharon

Stone; this thought keeps him pressed up against it, which helps to correct his sloppy posture. The list goes on.

Every person I work with has his or her own personal list of "secrets." Many wouldn't think of leaving home without them! For example, my dear friend, Gus Lee, a best-selling Asian-American author, won't go on tour without his notes; he keeps them in his wallet and refers to them right before every appearance.

You may think that an actor simply receives the script for his or her current role, learns the lines, and then performs them. No, it's not that simple. Most good actors employ coaches who help them "work" those lines — coaches, teachers, and directors who give actors the "tricks and secrets" that allow them to reach into the heart and soul of the character they're playing.

Now, what about average people, terrified at the thought of getting up in front of an audience, who have all they can handle let alone devising some little head games to improve their performances? If this describes you, the "tricks and secrets" I've mentioned may be necessary in order for you to be at your best when speaking to an audience. It doesn't mean that you're being phony, or that you've suddenly become an entirely different person. To the contrary. What it does mean is that you've been able to con yourself into believing certain thoughts that allow you to display yourself to the best possible advantage.

I mentioned in an earlier chapter that I often pretend I'm speaking to my daughter, Shannon, when I'm in front of a group. She thinks I'm fabulous, so I'm not self-conscious at all about what I do or say in front of her; I'm the most free when I'm with her. If I simply imagine that everyone in the audience is Shannon, then I really go for it. And it's then that I give the audience my personal best, and share my true self, without pretense. In order to be effective and to sell to my audience, I know that I need to be who I really am. So in a very roundabout way — by pretending I'm talking to someone else — I end up talking to the audience in the most connectable way possible, from my most human side.

I hope this new information about building a character is not misleading to you. Earlier in the book, I stated very adamantly that in order to be our best selves, we need to be who we really are, and not try to be somebody else. The concept of "tricks and secrets" is not designed to make you over into someone else; rather, it allows you to add bits and pieces of positive characteristics borrowed from others, or makes you think "different time, different place, different thing" in order to reveal *you* at your best.

Here are some of the other "secrets" that I use quite often: When I'm with a crowd where I feel intimidated, I pretend I'm some major movie star like Jane Fonda. The group is probably very honored to be with me! If I want to keep my posture erect, I tell myself I'm a ballet dancer. To keep my face animated in an interesting way, I imagine that a camera is following me, and I have to register certain feelings with my features in case the audio breaks down. If I want to use all the range and quality of my voice, I think of myself on a London stage doing Shakespeare. If I'm afraid of not making the sale, I tell myself I've just won the lottery, so getting the sale is no big deal; I don't need it.

Most of my personal "tricks and secrets" remain fairly standard wherever I go, whomever I'm with. However, there are some special performance adjustments I use on a regular basis. Depending on the situation or the audience, there are times when I rearrange, add to, or delete these adjustments. For example, if a room is small and intimate, I probably won't need to throw my voice like when I'm pretending to be on the London stage. If I'm pitching to a group of Japanese businessmen, I might tone myself down and appear a bit more submissive and soft. (In that instance, my "secret" might be to imagine that I'm Melanie Griffith.) When I'm speaking as a keynote motivator, I might think "basketball coach." If I'm called upon to give a talk on humor, I might think "Whoopi Goldberg," "Ellen DeGeneres," or "Paula Poundstone."

These all work very well for me. Before I make an appearance in one of the capacities I've mentioned above, I evaluate my "tricks and secrets" and decide how I'm going to play the part. In other words, I call upon my repertoire — my own collection of what works for me — and imprint those images on my mind before I take the stage.

Remember: Every performance, every speech, every presentation you give is as distinctively different as each role in a play or motion picture. As a result, you may have to adapt yourself accordingly, like I do.

My primary goal in assigning "tricks and secrets" to my students is to ensure that they punch up their strengths and eliminate their weaknesses. Everybody has both gifts and flaws; everybody is different. The idea is to play with the differences, highlighting people's gifts and downplaying their flaws, so they can present themselves in the best light possible, as the unique individuals they are.

Everyone can play this "character" game. It's fun. It's powerful. It makes you versatile. It gives you depth. It provides you with comfort and ease. Most of all, however, it brings out the best in you. And as I've already said, if you're scared, it gives you something to hide behind — a mask to wear and then discard when you don't need it any more.

To recap, then, by using the "tricks and secrets" I've suggested, you end up playing a "character." And even though you may be temporarily hiding behind this character, the irony is that you've actually become the best that you can be.

Maybe you're someone who doesn't need this type of side coaching. Then, again, this approach may provide a cure-all for the jitters and/or the frustrating inability to tap into your personal greatness.

If you want to experiment with making up a list of your own "tricks and secrets," try the following:

1. See if you can first identify your fears, shortcomings, bad habits, and deficiencies. In doing so, you'll create a starting point for building your character. Assess the categories we've covered in this book. Does your vocal production need attention? Is your energy level too low? Are you unable to self-express? Does fear block you from being your most relaxed and comfortable self? To clarify this, make a list.

2. You can easily videotape and/or audiotape yourself and review the tape. Be your own director and make a list of the strengths and weaknesses of the "character" you see.

3. Now that you've identified the pros and cons — what you've got, what you're lacking — see if you can assign a "secret" to each one. For instance, if you constantly say "uh" and "um," your "secret" might be that you'll swallow them (like

when you were caught chewing gum in school) before you utter them. Whatever mind-set you choose, it will help you to first become aware, and then force you to change the thing that needs changing. It's different for each one of us. For personal power and strength, you may want to conjure up the memory of your favorite actor, hero, or business executive. I think "Ingrid Bergman" or "Faye Dunaway" for strength, "Liza Minnelli" for friendliness, "Sally Field" for believability, and "Tom Hanks" for earthiness. Even the simple identification and appreciation of positive qualities you see in others is a start in reshaping your delivery; you're focusing on a different way of "acting" than you have previously. In addition, when we study others, we begin to mirror them.

4. Don't pile on too much too quickly. Try a few new "tricks" first and lock them in. Then for the next speech or presentation, add another. Then another. The idea is to add a little at a time, nailing each one into your subconscious mind. Pretty soon, like the other strategies you've learned in the "Miller" book, these "tricks and secrets" will become automatic responses, especially when you're under pressure.

5. Allow yourself weeks and even months for weaving your "character tapestry." Like any great work of art, it takes time and effort. Don't get discouraged if you try to give yourself a mental adjustment but lose track of it. Also, don't be discouraged if you slip back into former, less than complimentary tendencies. The awareness alone is a big step, and in time, you'll feel the "tricks and secrets" beginning to take precedence over your previous bad habits.

6. If you can find a coach to work with you until you reach your desired level of performance, do so. There's nothing like having an objective eye and a cheerleader, too!

7. Take a "character" class in an acting or improv program. This will give you the freedom to really explore — at no risk to yourself — various personality traits. As a result of such study, you're more likely to be open to making changes and getting out of your self.

8. Most important of all, be willing to pretend. It's only by making a commitment to do so that you can explore your imagination and be open to all your talents and resources.

9. Don't feel guilty about putting on a mask at your performances. Remember: Great actors do it all the time. There's nothing wrong with insulating yourself from what you perceive as threatening and confining. And if you're speaking in front of people, it's natural to want to feel safe and secure, knowing that you're giving them the very best *you* possible.

Chapter 20

Don't Write It
— Microwave It

The "Square Within a Square" Theory

Tell the truth about something: Do you prepare fully for your speech or presentation? By that I mean, do you memorize your material and rehearse it thoroughly? Of course not. Most people don't, so you shouldn't feel guilty. Fortunately, though, there is a way to package your speech, presentation, or sales pitch that's both fast and easy. (Now, there are two words we love to hear!)

In working with business professionals, I've learned a great deal about how people prepare for a speech or presentation. The majority of my work has been with people who regularly make speeches before audiences of a few hundred, or presentations and sales pitches before small groups. Most of these professionals don't spend much time at all getting ready. The only exceptions seem to be when they're giving those once-a-year big speeches before hundreds of people when someone's job (usually their own!) is on the line. I'm not saying that every executive falls into the "barely prepared" trap, but at least 90 percent of the business professionals I've coached over the years simply will not take the time to adequately prepare for those important moments — at least not in the same way a full pro performer would.

Here's the typical scenario: If it's one of those lengthy written speeches, the average business professional will wait until the last minute to even look it over. Often, they'll spend most of their speaking time simply reading the speech to the audience. If you've been unlucky enough to be an audience member during one of those talks, you'll have noticed that no two lines are read convincingly. And frequently, you spend the entire time looking at the top of the speaker's head. Speakers and presenters like this almost always bore us, because they're not what we call good "cold readers." How can they possibly connect to an audience when they aren't even connected to their own material?

On the other hand, there are those few speakers who do prepare, and sometimes even over-prepare. They memorize the text of their speech, and then deliver it like they're reading instructions on how to make toll-house cookies. They know their stuff, but often the material is bulky, verbose, redundant, and has no punch.

And then there are those presenters who just get up with no preparation whatsoever, no notes, and just wing it. They fling messages hither and yon, meander all over the place, constantly lose their train of thought, repeat themselves, and attempt to hide their insecurity with clever buzz words and phrases that mean nothing to us. I call these folks the "macho brigade." They have a lot of moxie, usually love to hear themselves talk, and for some reason tend to sound louder than everybody else. They might be a bit more interesting than the "read-my-speech" type of speaker, but when they've finished speaking, you're not able to make much sense out of what you've just heard. Ironically, I don't think they can either!

Speakers and presenters who use these three styles of organizing information are probably not going to get the reaction they were hoping for from their audiences, nor are their audiences getting what they need. Nobody wins.

Ergo, the "Square Within A Square" theory. It's a method that allows for adequate preparation and clear messages. It's been proven to work, and requires only about 20 minutes of effort. What I like most about it, though, is that it allows individuals to improvise most of their speeches and presentations. This ties back into the concept of being in sync with yourself, a tenet of the "Miller" philosophy that we discussed earlier.

Here's how the "Square Within A Square" theory works. First, we start with the assumption that most of us won't be asked to speak about something we don't already know about, so why should we write everything down? (Except, of course, when we must keep tabs on statistics.) Composing a speech or presentation word-by-word is time consuming; besides, how we write is often not how we speak. We want to converse *with* the audience. We don't want to sound like a textbook, or like we're reading a recipe. But if we write out the speech and then deliver it from the written text, we often sound formal and detached. Bor-ing! So given that we're going to be talking about a subject that's familiar to us, all we really need is some kind of written outline.

That's where the "Square Within A Square" method comes to your aid, and here's how it works. First, you identify your theme. Most people will spend a lot of time on this, but that's okay. This identification process — pinpointing your theme — helps you to tailor the subsequent information so that it's easy for the audience to assimilate. It also helps to keep your message clear, to the point, and — most important of all — interesting.

Many people discover when they first examine their content that they have two or three themes, or several ideas that they want to impart. However, if you're there at the podium to inform, educate, or even persuade, you'd better get real focused on what you want to say. Having too many "main" points only confuses you, and your audience as well. But once you've identified the central and main point you want to make (i.e., your theme), you're already halfway home! Hooray!

A reasonable guideline for locating your theme is to ask yourself, "What would I want them to remember if I only had ten seconds to sum up the gist of my message?" Another strategy for getting at your theme is to think of your speech as either an AP or UPI type newspaper story, in which the headline tells it all (for instance, "Dog Bites Man"), or as a motion picture film, in which the film's title gives you the general idea of what's to come ("When Harry Met Sally").

Your main theme will trigger all the subsequent material you'll need in order to support your overall message. If it helps, you can think of your theme as an advertising slogan; your theme is whatever phrase contains the main message, what-

"SQUARE WITHIN A SQUARE" EXAMPLE

Theme: Everyone Is A Performer, But Few People Are Trained To Be
(1-hour speech)

I. Intro

7 min.

- Execuprov is
- Born – *Friendly*
- Who Coach – *Story Telling*
- Stars – *Matter of Fact*
- Story (Punchline) – *Fun*

II. Basics

6 min.

- Breathing – *Free*
- Diction – *Firm*
- Concentration – *Mysterious*
- Awareness – *Pensive*
- Demo (Punchline)

III. Other Skills

18 min.

- Mental Agility – *Energetic*
- Energy – *Enthusiastic*
- Emotion – *Desperate*
- Listening – *Intense*
- Give & Take – *Patient*
- Refusal/Denial – *Concerned*
- Body Language – *Cynical*
- Timing/Spontaneity – *Upbeat*
- Story (Punchline) – *Fun*

IV. What's So Funny

8 min.

- Humor in Talks – *Serious*
- Gauge Audience – *Intellectual*
- Writing It – *Enthused*
- Delivery – *Funny*
- Homework – *Serious*
- Demo (Punchline)

V. Square within Square

10 min.

- Chart – *Matter of Fact*
- AP Story/Film – *Light*
- Jane, Dick, Spot – *Fun*
- 20 Min. – *Patient*
- Story (Punchline)

VI. Summary

10 min.

- Dos/Don'ts – *Compassionate*
- E.P. Classes – *Direct*
- Questions – *Friendly*
- Quote (Punchline)

ever you're there to talk about. Starting off your presentation by announcing up front what the audience needs to know, and telling them from the outset what you're up to, will successfully "situate" your audience. When an audience is situated, they're comfortable; and when they're comfortable, they can begin to absorb your "pitch," whatever it is.

Your theme has now become your "headline" or your "movie title" or your "advertising slogan." It has also become the large, or outside, "square" on the "Square Within A Square" diagram. Inside that large square, you can begin to "square off" your "sub-headlines" or "film scenes." Each square within the larger square will then contain bulleted words or catch-phrases that trigger your thoughts. Let me give you an example.

Let's say I'm doing a speech, and my main theme is:

Theme: Everyone Is A Performer, But Few People Are Trained To Be.

My first sub-headline or scene is my **introduction (I. Intro)**. Within that square, I'm going to write down several buzz words that will trigger the points I want to make as I introduce myself and talk about my reason for being there. I'm going to talk about **what ExecuProv is, how ExecuProv came to be, who I've trained, why I do it,** and **how it works.**

When I get to my first phrase, **"ExecuProv is,"** I'm going to explain what the program is all about, how it came to be, and what the overall "Miller" theory is.

When I glance at the word **"Born,"** it will remind me to talk about now natural and spontaneous we all were in our early years; how easy it was then to communicate our needs improvisationally.

"Who Coach" is a phrase that helps me to remember to tell the audience about my various clients, the companies I've worked for, and a few interesting experiences.

"Stars" is the recall button for me to talk about how celebrities are also uncomfortable, and how and what they do to train for their performances.

The word **"Story (Punchline)"** is my cue to give the "punchline" or final comment to my introduction. I usually share an interesting story about one of my students or a behind-the-scenes story about a major star. Then I move on to the next square.

In order to drive home to the audience my main point or theme, I'm going to repeat it as I go along, whenever appropriate, as well as when I reach the end of that square and every square thereafter. In addition, before leaving each square, I'm going to end my comments with a "punchline." Now, a punchline doesn't have to be a joke; instead, it can be a quote, a bit of philosophy, a humorous story, a demonstration, an anecdote, a famous saying, a moral...it can even be a personal experience.

As you go about organizing your talk, assign each square its own punchline. Your audience will love it. Even more importantly, the audience will remember what you had to say, rather than forgetting the contents of your speech or presentation just a few minutes after it's over.

Punchlines make your speech memorable, and allow you to make your points in a vivid fashion. They also help to bring your segments, or squares, to completion. In addition, the use of punchlines gives your audience the opportunity to digest the information in each segment, and to clear their mental palates before you move on to your next point, or square; and it helps you to be direct and concise in each portion of your talk.

The "Square Within A Square" method spares you the redundancy that often occurs with speakers who aren't using an outline, who keep going over the same information again and again. The number of points you want to make will determine the number of smaller squares within the large, overall square. Remember: Keep it simple.

Within the large schematic drawing, you'll notice that I've included six squares containing the points I want to make. On the diagram, too, you'll note that next to each bulleted word I've included a word that suggests a "mood." This allows me to stay interesting, because I'm going to be varying my "attitude" as I go through my talk, from one point to the next. As you'll recall, contrast and variety are what keep us interesting to our audience — no matter what size the group.

What makes great actors really *great* is the ability to segue quickly and surprisingly from one mood to another. In doing so, they punctuate their performances and give their characters more complexity. As a result, their audiences are fascinated. On the other hand, if you deliver your speech using the same mood throughout, your audience will soon tune you out. As I mentioned earlier, when you fly in an airplane, right away you notice the sound of the engine; but after a period of time, you don't notice that sound any more — not because the sound goes away, but because it becomes "normal" for you to hear it. Well, the same thing occurs when you deliver a talk in just one mood all the way through, no matter what the mood is — enthusiasm, boredom, or anything in between.

I repeat: Any delivery that stays the same will become monotonous, and more often than not, the audience will become bored because of it. Don't forget that your job is to entertain. You want to take people for a ride. You can do that by frequently changing your mood to correspond appropriately to the subject matter; it always works. We talked about this in Chapter 14 when we covered self-expression. Once again, jotting down mood reminders next to your buzz words will help you move around emotionally during your talk. The bottom line is, your audience will follow along, and THEY WILL STAY TUNED IN!

Referring back to the diagram, you'll see that to the right of each square there's a number. This number indicates the amount of time I've allotted myself for covering the material in each square. Some people have a tendency to ramble on at the beginning of their speeches, or to digress at length when they hit a key point. When you have a given period of time in which to deliver your presentation (and that's true for most of us), you want to make sure that you allocate ample time to each square so that you can cover the information adequately. I know many speakers who express deep remorse after their speeches because they didn't have time to cover everything. If you keep your talk well managed in terms of allocating time, then you'll experience a sense of control and will be able to hit all the salient points before your time is up.

Now, when it comes to laying out the speech, you can put the whole thing on one piece of paper, like in the schematic, or you can put each square on a 3x5 card. Most of my students seem to prefer the cards, because that way, they're only dealing with one segment of their speech or presentation at a time, and when they've completed a "square," they can just toss that card aside and move on.

Here are some important points with regard to the "Square Within A Square" theory and method:

1. Remember, your audience will forget approximately 80 percent of what you say within 30 minutes of leaving your presentation. Knowing this, you'll want to ask yourself: What is the single most important message I want to leave with them? This, of course, is the one sentence or phrase that identifies your theme.

2. When you think of your main theme, think of it in terms of a slogan, a tagline, a headline ("Dog Bites Man"), or a film title ("When Harry Met Sally").

3. Repeat your theme frequently throughout your talk, especially at the end of each "square" and wherever else you think it fits. Again, this may be the only message that "sticks" with your audience. Also, it's a great way to stall if you do get off track. You can simply reiterate your theme until you collect yourself.

4. On a single piece of paper, lay out your speech "squares" so that the smaller speech squares fit within the large, overall square that represents your theme. Then put each "inside" square on a separate 3x5 card, listing your subheads, buzz words, mood words, phrases, and punchlines. For easy reference, you might also want a separate 3x5 card for any important stats or numbers you'll be using. Each card provides quick access to all your information and is easy to follow.

5. With regard to your "inside" squares, think of them like subheads in an AP or UPI story, or think of each square as a scene in a film. Build your "story" or "film" so that it has continuity, interest, flair, and provides important information. And just like a news story or film, make sure that it has a beginning, middle and end.

6. After you're prepared all your cards, stand before the mirror and run through your speech a couple of times. Yes, it takes only about 20 minutes to prepare the "Square Within

A Square" format, but it may take a bit more time to rehearse your presentation. But just like polished performers, you'll want to prepare; so take the necessary time. Plan ahead.

7. While you're rehearsing and then when you finally deliver your presentation/speech/sales pitch, make sure that you don't filter what you say. Let your mind lead you. Trust yourself. Let go. IMPROVISE!!! Know that each time you give the same presentation some of your material may vary, but that's okay. You want to stay fresh and interesting, and as long as you cover the most important points (those listed in your inside squares), you'll be fine. Remember this very important "Miller" fact: Most of us won't ever be asked to speak on a topic about which we know nothing! Let it flow. Another note here: When you improvise, you'll stimulate a higher energy level and better self-expression, and you'll stay more conversational and say more interesting things to your audience. In fact, it's during those spontaneous moments, when your delivery is natural and genuine, that you often say the most brilliant and creative things.

8. Make sure you assign a different emotion to each inside square as your trigger word or phrase. Varying your moods will help keep your audience tuned in. Remember, it's contrast and variety that keep us interesting to others.

9. As a precaution, figure out the number of minutes in your talk you want to devote to each square. This will keep you from running out of time, and eliminate having to rush through the final moments of your speech because you lost track of time. Find a timepiece you can count on; in other words, bring a watch to the podium, or make sure there's a clock nearby (even at the back of the room) so that you can keep on course.

10. Keep your remarks simple and easy to assimilate. (Think "Jane, Dick and Spot.") One way to assess this is to ask yourself: "If I walked in off the street, came to the wrong room and listened in on this speech, would I understand it?" If the answer is "no," you've missed the mark; you're probably getting too complicated. Remember this: The reason that people over-explain things is often because they're

afraid of being misunderstood. However, we're inundated with information every day; we have too much input and not enough gray matter. So if you want your message to be remembered, keep it simple, concise, clear, direct, to the point. Expositional dialogue is often a bore.

11. When you deliver, stay conversational and human.

12. Get in touch with your "motivation." Why are you doing what you're doing? If we don't have a passion for our work, it will show. Always check your motivation before going on; great performers do, every time.

13. Have fun. Enjoy yourself. Remember: Nobody gives your speech/presentation/sales pitch quite like you do. You're one of a kind. Share your magic with your audience!

Be patient, because the first couple of times you try this new way of organizing your material, it may take some maneuvering, rearranging, and additional thinking in order to find that main theme; and it will probably require you to have a different mind-set in order to get used to doing things in a new way. But just think about how much more interesting you'll be. Think about your audience. Think about what you want the end result to be!

Chapter 21

Humor Me

Everybody's Funny

You may think I'm nuts, but I believe everyone is funny — funny in his or her own way perhaps, but nonetheless, funny. Call it an act of nature, a miracle, whatever you want, but it's true: A sense of humor is a God-given gift. Many people don't use theirs, but it's there in all of us.

Some of us laugh a lot every day, others laugh sporadically, and still others laugh only on rare occasions. What's true for all of us, though, is that we don't laugh often enough; and we don't bring out the humor in those around us either. It's been said that, on average, children laugh about 200 times a day; adults, seven. How sad.

I think the reason that adults laugh so seldom is because we live in a difficult world. We're bombarded daily with disturbing information; we're stressed and consumed with too many all-important tasks. There's no time for humor.

The harder life is, though — the state of the world, our personal circumstances, etc. — the more we *NEED* to be able to laugh. In fact, I think we should all regard ourselves as humor ambassadors and do our best to spread good cheer, *especially* during our speeches, presentations, and sales pitches, and also during all of our daily business activities. Our good cheer can evoke smiles or even deep, convulsive belly-benders. Besides love, there's nothing more universal than humor. If you want to "win" over somebody, be funny. You'll soon find that there's nothing more bonding than humor.

Laughter is certainly MY salvation. I lecture and teach classes on the subject of "Humor In The Workplace," in which I ask my students to make a list of the specific things they can do every day to exercise their sense of humor — or maybe to get in touch with the fact that they do have one. After all, if you can identify your own sense of humor, you'll then be able to integrate different forms of humor into your speeches, presentations, business meetings, etc. But again, the first step is to realize that you *HAVE* a sense of humor.

Humor is all around us. Many of the trying situations we find ourselves in are usually funny — later on, that is (sometimes much later on!). There are incidents that can seem tragic (or difficult, stressful, frustrating, frightening, etc.) at the time, but when we tell someone else about them, these same events often become humorous. I love Woody Allen's definition of comedy: "Time plus tragedy equals comedy. If it bends, it's funny; if it breaks, it isn't."

In addition to traumatic events, we often encounter regular, everyday situations that are just plain funny and worth repeating. It's through this transfer of information that we start to learn the art of storytelling, which puts us in touch with our ability to convey humor; so everyone, then, can take these stories and share them with an audience.

In my speeches, I often share some of my experiences. For example, I have told several audiences about the time I was going through a traumatic divorce and having a terrible time keeping my mind on my work. At that particular time, I was running a large public relations agency. During a therapy session one day, I excused myself to use the bathroom, and subsequently discovered that the waistband of my triangular-shaped underwear was wrapped around my left thigh, with the left leg hole around my waist. I burst out laughing. (Thank God no one was in the stall next to me!) Apparently, I was so preoccupied with my grief that morning while getting dressed, I couldn't even manage to put my underwear on straight.

That incident has remained an important symbol to me, because it made me realize that even on the worst of days, I could still find something to laugh about. It also reassured me that I still had a sense of humor. (I think we get so intense sometimes that we forget that.) To this day, when things aren't going well, I tend to wear my underwear in that uncharacteristic fashion, because I know it will trigger a little levity; it still makes me laugh. In fact, the retelling of the underwear fiasco is often the way I open my humor speeches. It's a great icebreaker!

As you begin to explore your own sense of humor, I challenge you to recall an incident that was embarrassing to you. When you do, it should make you smile or laugh out loud. If you're at all human (and have lived a few decades), you probably have several unforgettable stories like this.

Here's another challenge: On a small card, write down some buzz words that will trigger a humorous memory. Refer to it frequently, especially on a bad day. Keep adding to the card. Soon you'll have a diary of humorous events that will serve as a ready source of material for your speeches and presentations.

For easy reference, I myself keep an ongoing list of some of the funny things I've experienced or created, or that have happened to others. Here's one: On my 35th birthday I held a surprise party for myself! I sent out invitations asking everyone to arrive at 7:30 p.m. and park down the street so I wouldn't see their cars. I made my entrance at 8:00 p.m., my guests yelled "Surprise!", and I screamed something like "I don't believe this!"

Here's another one: When I first started my own business (literally in a closet next to my bedroom), I felt a little isolated and lonely; I was the only one in the "office." So I talked myself into a Christmas party and then a gift exchange. I drew my own name, of course, and got myself a great present. During that Christmas party, I also gave myself a bonus! It was great fun, and again, provided me with another interesting story to tell.

I have one client who thought he was the most unfunny person in the world. When he finally caught on to the secret of simply recounting some of his most embarrassing moments, and then got big laughs, he became a humor addict. Now he won't do a speech without it. I have a speech where I just tell the audience one story after another about some of the dumb things I've done — like the time I did the second half of my grocery shopping with somebody else's cart, or the time I took half of a tablecloth to the podium with me.

When I recount those embarrassing — but now humorous — moments, it makes my audience realize that I'm fallible and human, and puts them at ease; it creates an opening for me to gently connect to my audience.

In other words, the use of humor disarms my audience and makes them more receptive to my "pitch." Plus, I've entertained them.

I confess, there are those who argue that not everyone IS funny. But I'm not buying it. You see, even cynics can't deny that something funny has happened to them at some point in their lives. All they need to do, then, is learn how to recount those stories in an interesting way.

What I find really sad is that some people have never fully developed themselves in the humor area. If you want to borrow a term from human development or growth, you'd say these people are "stunted." Somewhere along the way, they shut down or withdrew; their lack of humor became a habit, a pattern.

Well, if you think you're in this category, take heart: The remainder of this chapter and the one following are designed to help you understand what humor is, why and how something is funny, and how to inject humor into your speeches and presentations. The "Miller" goal is to get you to bring forth your own sense or humor, and to encourage you to use it wherever you go, whatever you do. And you can begin with the "funny or embarrassing moment" assignment as an awareness exercise, to remind yourself that you definitely *are* funny.

Now, let me back up just a bit to provide some additional insight into how I arrived at my insistence that everyone is funny. I didn't just sit under a tree or on a mountaintop to postulate the "everybody's funny" theory; the proof of it came from the years I spent watching comedians, studying average speakers/presenters, and, most importantly, closely analyzing the components of improv comedy. In addition, my research included conferring with a number of experts in the field of comedy — directors, writers, performers — who assisted me in defining what makes humor, *humor*. Eventually, I decided to take all the information I'd accumulated and pass it on, in an easy-to-assimilate manner, to the business execs I was coaching.

When I began teaching the humor thing to those business people, they confided in me that the most difficult aspect of humor was that their funny moments were a hit-and-miss proposition. They weren't ready to believe that every time they got up to speak, their jokes or stories would work with the audience.

After carefully considering their fears, I arrived at the following conclusion — and you might want to decide if this applies to you: Many executives seem to be the left brainers (the more analytical types), so they need to be approached in a more linear fashion. In order to do that, I dissected what I believe to be the major components of humor, separating out the individual components, and explained the nature of each of those components to my students. Then I devised a method that allowed them to weave together the components in order to "comprise" humor. It was kind of like a chemistry project. If they added one compound to the next, then to the next, and so on, the ultimate formula would allow for a big blast — of humor.

After my students and I had analyzed humor, I asked them to study different kinds of comedy and different styles of comedians; for example, I had them compare the low-key style of Charles Grodin to the frenetic style of Richard Lewis. They were also directed to watch network sitcoms, and to jot down what they liked and didn't like, what made them laugh and what didn't, and why. Next, I had them review their journals of funny experiences, the notes they'd been keeping. My students began to see that humor was all around them, and they became aware of opportunities to create and to share humor. Ultimately, each one gave in and admitted that he or she did, after all, have a sense of humor. They also admitted that they each had their own unique humor "style," and came to appreciate that they could use their humor gift whenever they wanted to.

So, the moral of this chapter is that you, too, can develop your humor muscle and use it to spice up your speech or presentation when appropriate, or when you happen to feel like it. First, you need to understand what constitutes humor. After that, you can go about the task of putting together some humor, and then integrating the funny stuff into your speeches and presentations. And you can do so consistently, effectively, and most importantly, with confidence in the results. Remember, you're not expected to be Billy Crystal, Danny DeVito, Whoopi Goldberg, or Bette Midler. All you need to be is you! You can be funny!

Chapter 22

WHAT'S SO FUNNY?

How, When and Where to Get Humor Into Your Talk

In the previous chapter I touched on the idea that everyone loves to hear stories. We grew up at our parents' knees listening to them; their stories grabbed and held our attention, and, of course, we especially liked the funny ones. The thing to remember is that when you're center stage, you're more or less in that parental position. Your audience is waiting for your story. Some of the most dynamic and energizing speakers I've seen were the ones who told one story after another. What if you're not a major speechmaker, or you do mainly presentations and sales pitches? It doesn't matter. Getting up before people at the podium or the meeting table, it's all the same thing. When you're presenting anything, good stories almost always work — especially the funny ones.

So, the first suggestion I have for you is that when you go about compiling your material, be sure to include an interesting story or a humorous moment. Believe it or not, every story you tell can be funny, even the tragic ones. (Remember the last chapter?) Once again, the tragic stories are often the most hilarious, in retrospect. As you may already know, life's ills provide the basis for the material of most well-known comics.

Stories that get a great response from the audience are most often told with a genuine and authentic delivery. That delivery is what makes them so funny. And the more real you are, the funnier you'll be. So I don't care what your speech is about, whether the content is serious or otherwise: Think of humor like air; it's something you need around you, all the time. (In fact, wouldn't it be great if the FDA or somebody else made humor one of the basic food groups for the mind?)

Now, let's get started on analyzing what humor is. We talked a little about that in the previous chapter. My theory is that there are five major components that make up this thing called humor: energy, self-expression, timing, spontaneity, and attitude. *If all of these are working fully together, any joke or story you tell will get a positive response.* On the other hand, if you display any pretense, formality, filtering, phoniness, or any of the other problems that can interfere with *YOUR* natural "synchronization," you're not going to be your *SELF*. As a result, your material may not work, or it may work only some of the time (remember when we talked about humor as a hit-or-miss proposition).

In any analysis of the five components of humor, we should always begin with energy, since energy is the power that drives your "joke" or story. For your material to work, your energy field must be strong. Think of your personal energy as the fuel that drives the rocket. It's the boost that will launch your story; it's what gives power and punch to your delivery. It's hard to tell a joke well when your energy level is down or "at ease." When you cook, you turn on the heat. So fire up and turn on the heat before you make your presentation. And make sure that you keep revving all the way, especially at those points in your jokes or stories when you're building momentum.

Self-expression — boosted by energy — is also essential in humorous story telling. *Remember, it's not what you say; it's how you say it.* The emotion that you attach to each segment of your story will serve to punctuate the point. For instance, I had a student who told a story about going to a trucking convention. He wanted to be cool, he told us, like the other attendees, and they were all wearing cowboy boots; so he, too, bought a pair and proudly put them on. Later that same night, though, when he tried to remove them, he couldn't get the boots off. His wife was no help: She'd had one too many and had passed out face down on the bed.

As my student went along telling his story, he included a

blow-by-blow description of every attempt he made to get those boots off. (He finally ended up prying the heels loose by pressing the back end of each boot against the elbow bend of the pipe underneath the bathroom sink in his hotel room!).

Although this story reads humorously now, when my student first told it, he sounded like he was giving driving directions. None of us laughed (though we sort of smiled). Then, when he began to put emotion into his telling of it, the story came alive, and we couldn't *stop* laughing. He let us know what he was *FEELING* every step of the way. We *felt* it with him. We traveled through each event of the ordeal, from amusement to frustration to embarrassment to desperation. As he changed his moods, we did, too; we actually took the emotional ride with him. We lived the experience as if we were right there in the hotel room with him. It was very, *very* funny!

Whenever you recount an experience and express your innermost thoughts and feelings during each moment of that experience, it's always funny. You also become vulnerable. Audiences love that. You really captivate your audience, even if the audience is only one person. In fact, allowing yourself to be vulnerable is a genuine and honest way to communicate. We humans love to see that from other humans. And there is something about all of it that always makes us laugh, too. I suppose it's because we're relating to the feelings and thoughts being expressed. You see it in stand-up acts all the time.

So far, we've talked about energy and self-expression as components of humor. Number three in the countdown is spontaneity. It's the key factor in making a story humorous; in fact, it's probably the single most important element. When you let the story or the joke come out of your mouth "NATURALLY," when the words just pour out and there's no pre-planning, you tend to say fascinating and often very funny things. As I mentioned in an earlier chapter, most business people are not good with scripts; but when they shoot from the hip — just tell it like it is — that's when the humor works.

Think of it this way: You wouldn't recount a humorous experience to your best friend over the phone or at a restaurant from a memorized script, would you? You see, when we're talking to people we're comfortable with, we just tell it like it is —

or was. That's what's so interesting to the listener. We need to use more of that same conversational, spontaneous dialogue and delivery when telling stories during our speeches and presentations. Talk about a great way to connect!

You're probably thinking, well, that's fine, but how can I remember my jokes and stories when I'm up in front of an audience? In improv comedy, we travel from the beginning of a piece of work to the end via "beats," which are best defined as pivotal points or segue moments in a scene. The audience will tell us who the players are, what they're doing, and what the conflict is. From there, the actor develops the scene by improvising, or filling in the blanks. The scene progresses from one stage to the next, with each major change within the scene being termed a "beat point." Similarly, if we're telling a humorous story during a speech or presentation, we only need to remember the "beats" or "highlights" of that experience, and then easily fill in the actualities by improvising.

Think of beats as an outline. It's all you ever really need. I teach a class called "What's So Funny?". I ask each student to bring an interesting story (some life experience) to share with the rest of the class. First, the students tell the stories their own way. Later on, they retell the stories, this time incorporating the five components of humor. As I "work" their stories, I help them identify where those strategic "beat points" should fall. Again, beats are, quite simply, the high points of the story, the key occurrences along the way from beginning to end. You can tell the same joke or story many times, and each time it'll probably be somewhat different. That's not just okay; that's great! Each time you tell it, it'll become more interesting to you. And if it's more interesting to you, it will be interesting to your audience as well. If you rely on "beats," you'll perpetuate — and even guarantee — your own spontaneity. This will also help you with another aspect of storytelling: the build.

What's the build? It's the momentum that carries the story along. When you stay spontaneous, you usually get caught up in your own energy because you're *in the moment* — in other words, you're reliving, or living, the joke or story as it happened to you at the time. That's why every part of your story should get bigger and bigger as you take it from beginning to end. It's kind of the suspense thing, i.e., "...and then...and then...and then...and...then..." Many fairy tales are constructed in this fashion.

My belief is that when you have "build," you begin to create an atmosphere of expectancy, intrigue, and tremendous interest. If your remarks are spontaneous as they fall between the "beat points," the build mounts and people tend to stay tuned in. That's where the magic really comes in, when you improvise dialogue while telling the story — especially the "asides," those moments when you hit the parts of the story that reveal your *INNERMOST THOUGHTS AND FEELINGS* (THEY ARE *ALWAYS* FUNNY). **When you build on what you thought or felt at the time, you can use those thoughts and feelings as threads to weave your story together in a fascinating way.**

Now that you've got energy, self-expression, and spontaneity all going for you, you'll want to assure that everything else works by checking and/or fine-tuning your timing. This is critical. As a rule, this isn't something to think or worry about consciously. If you stay spontaneous, your own natural sense of timing will usually prevail. You can strengthen it, though, by doing the timing exercises in Chapter 15.

The next thing to do is to locate or create some one-liners to practice with. Now, read them several different ways to see which particular delivery sounds best to your ear. Notice which delivery FEELS right, too. There are a number of books available that contain jokes, funny quotes, and short (1-2 paragraphs) humorous stories that you can use for practice purposes. You can memorize your selections if you like, or you can try to remember just the beats and punchlines. Try them out in front of friends, a significant other, or better yet, your kids. Children are great barometers for what works. They don't even have to understand the content. If you're funny, they'll laugh. You can also tape record yourself; by listening to the playback, you'll *know* if your timing is right. Then try several different ways of delivering the stories or jokes. You might want to emphasize certain words one time, others the next. Experiment. Try the same joke or story in a variety of ways, and then pick the best "take."

Now, read a one-paragraph joke, grab the "beats," note the punchline, and then *paraphrase* it. (Don't memorize the joke.)

It's great practice for delivering your own stories — the kinds of experiences you tend to relay that you certainly aren't going to memorize or write down first. Some people are good at remembering jokes, and if you've ever been around chronic joke tellers (God forbid!), you'll notice that they usually tell their jokes differently each time. What's interesting about them is that they usually "color" a joke — add more descriptions, adjectives, etc. — each time they tell it. They provide graphic descriptions of scenery, feelings, characters...and it's downright spellbinding. (It must go back to that "Mom/Dad, read me a story" thing.)

Story tellers like those mentioned above almost always have a great sense of timing, because they usually "live" the story or joke as they're telling it. They are THERE. They're lost in it, and so are we! You do the same thing when telling a friend about an incident that was fascinating, exciting or funny. You often use the wait-until-you-hear-this approach. That's the same kind of timing you want to be using when you're up in front of that important audience, the one where you're making the do-or-die speech, presentation, or sales pitch.

The final element of timing is the punchline — the last phrase, sentence, or word in your joke or story. If the build is appropriate to the story, if you're living the event moment by moment and truly into what you're saying, the punchline will make for a natural big finish. Be sure that your punchline caps off the build, punctuates it (i.e., makes a point). In terms of timing, the way to ensure this terrific ending is to pause slightly before (and after) delivering the punchline. If you have several punchlines in a story or joke, provide pauses for each of them. However, the final punchline should get the biggest pause beforehand.

Think of your punchline as an island. It's out there all by itself, surrounded by water, not directly attached to anything. For a speaker, the punchline (the island) is surrounded by dead air — a pregnant pause that creates expectancy. You want that dead air (the pause) before and after each punchline to give it relevance and emphasis, and to give completion to your story or story segment. It's all in the timing; for instance, if you're nearing the end of a story, and you say, "And then he looked at his wife and said (PAUSE), "Don't say that to me, I did it yesterday." Don't forget, the pause is critical. You also need it after the delivery of the punchline, before you go on to the next story or joke. It tells the audience that you expect laughter or applause, or that you want them to get the point you're trying to make. They can digest it, find closure, get completion. If your timing is clean, you'll get a big laugh. Then you can move on.

The biggest problem in telling stories is nailing the punchline; but it's not that hard to do. Just give build to the story and air to the punchline. Remember, too, the longer the story, the bigger the payoff needs to be. In other words, the punchline or ending to your story will have to be strong enough to substantiate and support the material that preceded it. There is nothing worse than sitting through a big build-up only to have the closing remark — the point, the punchline — be weak. It's like a plane that climbs to a high altitude only to plunge downward nose-first. What a letdown. (I bet most plane crashes usually are, figuratively *and* literally!)

We've all heard speakers who let us down. I personally get hostile when this happens. After all, I sat there and listened attentively waiting for the payoff. I was good. I deserve something! So make sure your punchline is on a par with your story content. If your story goes on for some time, make sure you have several mini-punchlines as you plug along, and then BANG!, cap it off with a *big* finish. If your story is a short one, the demand on the punchline won't be as great. A good idea is to think about constructing your stories and jokes around the payoffs, so that your material will fit the circumstances and won't ever bomb.

To enrich your stories and jokes, you now want to add the final component of humor: attitude. *Webster's* defines attitude as a "feeling or emotion toward a fact or state." When you have "attitude," you clearly let the audience know where you're coming from. They know if you're feeling secure, inadequate, self-righteous, humble, determined, frivolous — there are hundreds of attitudes. This component is not to be confused with self-expression. Attitude is simply a device to give additional authenticity or overall meaning to your words, sentence by sentence. It's like the general "place" you're coming from.

Getting your intent across is a broader issue, and requires a definitive attitude. Attitude is the stand or position you take with regard to your overall subject matter. In an odd sense, it's *your* point of view. For instance, if you're interested in raising $4 million from a potential investment group, your overall attitude as you're speaking before them might be one of determination, or perhaps of desperation. Actually, it could be any one of a number of attitudes. Or, for another example, let's say you're sharing a story about the know-it-all mechanic who fixed your car; your attitude might be one of sarcasm. You see, the attitude is the "coming from" point of your story or joke telling.

Most of the stories you tell will have an origination point, and that's when your attitude gets established. What's your starting point? Are you gossiping? Are you angry? Are you compassionate? Are you carefree? In acting terminology, we refer to attitude as motivation. Actors will read their lines and then ask the director what their motivation is, in order to be able to establish an appropriate attitude.

Almost all attitudes can be humorous. And the more *incongruence* there is between the attitude and the material, the funnier the story or joke. For example, in a state (attitude) of great dignity, a woman might tell the story of her skirt falling off while she waited in line at the airport. I once told the story of finishing my grocery shopping with someone else's cart. My attitude as I recounted this embarrassing moment (blow-by-blow, incidentally) was one of great remorse. It worked, and people really laughed. My story could have been nothing more than a dull recollection, but I used attitude, self-expression, energy, and all my natural timing and spontaneity to put it across.

The good news is, if we follow the "Miller" formula, our humor will always work. We simply need to understand and integrate the five components that make humor, well, humor. After we get comfortable with injecting humor into our speeches, presentations, and sales pitches, we can reap the benefits of being funny — every time, all the time, whenever we choose.

Now that you have all the components that comprise humor and you understand how to implement them, you're probably asking yourself: "I know what constitutes humor, how to find my own, and how to deliver it; but where the hell do I put it?" The correct answer is wherever it feels right.

Finally, I strongly suggest you begin each presentation, speech, or sales pitch with a humorous comment or icebreaker. This allows you to immediately "smell" the audience, and provides an instant connection to everybody in the room. An icebreaker can be a joke, story, quote, or a question you ask the audience. And it can be delivered even before you introduce yourself. It warms up and situates the audience; it lets them know what you're up to, and gives them insight into your personality. I especially like to use humorous quips or icebreakers, because I want to know how far I can go with my humor with each particular group. But more importantly, I want people to know that I'm approachable and someone they're going to want to listen to and have fun with. As I mentioned previously, icebreakers can create an instant bond between you and your audience.

As you outline your speech, presentation, or sales pitch, take note of the many different places where you can insert an interesting case study, joke, personal experience, or fascinating story. Make an attempt to weave in humorous stories and remarks throughout your talk. If you concentrate on injecting humorous bits here and there, you'll delight your audience. You'll also find that these tidbits fit perfectly into your overall mosaic; and you'll wonder why you didn't start doing this a long time ago. It becomes just as much fun for you as it is for your audience. Remember how much everyone loves a good story. Even more importantly, remember how much everyone loves to laugh!

After you complete your speech outline, examine it to see whether there is a good balance between the serious content and the humor. Will people leave the room feeling entertained? Will they know you have a great sense of humor? Go ahead; I challenge you. What else do you want people to think and say about your work? Begin by incorporating humor slowly into your presentations. You'll gradually get the hang of it, and when you do, there's no going back! There's no bigger high than having people laugh at the funny things you say. Applause is nice, but laughter — well, why do you think there are so many stand-up comedians? Laughter means instant, obvious approval and acceptance. You deserve that, too. We all do!

The following are reminders, pointers, and homework assignments. They're geared to helping you explore your own sense of humor; to providing you with practical applications for it; and to giving you the tools and confidence so you'll want to express humor more often. And remember, your sense of humor is unique; no one else has one quite like yours. So share it. It's one of those gifts that keeps on giving!

1. There are five major components that make your humor "play": energy, self-expression, spontaneity, timing, and attitude. You need all five to get the job done. If one is missing, you'll be operating at a handicap.

2. Work daily on building your energy level. Pump it up before making that speech or talk. Pace or jabber; if you can't do these physically, then visualize yourself doing them. A strong energy output will supply your jokes with punch and power.

3. Self-expression exercises are also a daily must. The greater your emotional range, or mood variance, the funnier your delivery. As an analogy, the more you're able to tap into and express a variety of feelings, the more crayons you have available to you for coloring your stories.

4. Spontaneity can be increased by doing the flashcard exercises. They'll keep your mind agile and free. When we're spontaneous (on a roll), we're magical; people will latch on to us. When you're spontaneous, you'll also be perceived as confident and powerful.

5. Timing is critical in all things, especially in nature and in you. If your timing is off, nothing will "play." Discover your own cadence, your own natural rhythm. Experiment with one-liners and story telling. If your spontaneity is in "sync," your timing will gel; it will come naturally. Don't try to be someone you're not. Don't force your delivery. Notice the way you walk, the pitch of your voice; notice the rhythms around you. Everything has a beat to it. Develop your ear. Listen.

6. Remember, the longer the story, the bigger the payoff needs to be. Be prepared to support your story with a meaningful and hard-hitting punchline. It's like having a great dinner,

followed by a scrumptious dessert! Don't let the audience down. Your punchline should be the biggest and best part of your story. You should finish with a bang!

7. Keep your stories as close to the truth as possible. When people can relate to your experiences, they can laugh. If you recount your experiences in a fun way, you'll have people rolling in the aisles. Life is funny! Recap your day. It makes for great speech material when you share your personal experiences. Comics do this, and so do comedy writers. Your own frame of reference is best, because you were *there*! Talk about it; incorporate it into your talks.

8. When you practice jokes and stories that are already written down, read them in a variety of ways. Decide on the delivery that best suits your natural style. A great delivery will become automatic to you in a short period of time.

9. Assess your audience at the beginning of a talk by throwing out an icebreaker. This can be a joke, story, quote — anything that helps you connect. Icebreakers establish you as someone fun to be with, right up front.

10. When you tell your stories, jokes, and experiences, they are usually full of characters. Give your stories more dimension and color by making up different voices to go with each character's personality. As you speak *for* them, using different dialects and attitudes, it will help the audience distinguish the unique people in your tale.

11. Be sure there's air before and after each punchline to give impact, meaning, and closure to your stories or jokes.

12. Remember that every audience is different. Be spontaneous and flexible enough with your humor to play off of *them*. Don't assume that every audience will respond the same. Experiment. It will keep you fresh and on your toes.

13. Remember that each of us grew up at our mother's or father's knee listening to stories. Everybody warms up and tunes in when they sense a story coming. Stories are great for making a point and keeping people entertained. Your job is to entertain. If you entertain, you'll connect. If you connect, you'll sell.

14. LET YOUR MIND LEAD YOU. It's important to trust yourself *and* your sense of humor. Don't filter; that will only get in the way of your spontaneity. Be "in the moment" and allow your reactions to be direct responses to what is happening then and there. You frequently make funny, off-the-cuff remarks when you're in the company of close friends and others. Let it happen with everyone, everywhere.

15. Don't step on your laughs. When you first start to incorporate humor into your work, you might not be ready for the reaction. You don't expect it, so you just keep going. Remember, audience laughter is like an ocean wave. Hold until the minute the laughter seems to reach its peak. When it descends (subsides a bit), then continue talking again. Holding will become natural to you after a time. But be sure to wait until the laughter fades. You want to savor the moment; it's a real high. Comics say there's nothing better.

16. Study comedians. Watch their different styles of delivery, facial expressions, attitudes, and energy. Take notes and ask yourself what you liked or disliked about their performances. It will help you identify your own sense of humor. This will also assist you in analyzing why some people are funny, *WHY* humor works, and when.

17. Your audience will mirror you. If you're having a good time, they'll have a good time, too. If all the components of humor are in place, you'll be right down the center of yourself — your **BEST** self. The audience will pick that up, even unconsciously, and be right there with you. You can try to fake good humor and comedy, but the truth always seems to seep out; as a result, you'll get half-hearted laughter, polite laughter that doesn't feel genuine. Ask yourself: Did the joke you just delivered sound canned, contrived? You'll get back what you put out. If you're spontaneous, they'll be spontaneous. Don't fake it. Don't try. Just BE.

18. There's nothing more bonding than humor. It's universal and contagious. Stay healthy by including humor in your everyday life. It provides balance and endears you to people when you express it, especially in the workplace. It also re-

lieves stress, neutralizes tension, and gives you a better perspective.

19. Learn to laugh at yourself; it gives you more balance with the world and the things around you. It also provides some material for your talks!

20. Your sense of humor is a special gift; be generous with it. If you use humor, you'll probably get what you want. Don't cheat yourself. Humor can always carry you through that tough meeting, interview, speech, or presentation. We all know there are days when we need comic relief!

"Ah, yes, after all this training I feel like Sir Laurence Olivier.
Let's see, what is my motivation?"

Chapter 23

PUTTING IT OUT THERE

Dealing With the Media

If it's not your custom to deal with the media — be it electronic or print (radio or television; newspapers or magazines) — you can skip this chapter. However, if you're regularly called upon to interface with the media as an interview subject, then this chapter will be important.

I think the majority of people have a misconception about the media: They think that every media person is the same. In other words, if an interviewee regards those who work for the media as gods, then he or she will think all media people rank in that category. Alternatively, if the interviewee dislikes or distrusts even one media person, he or she will tend to feel that way about all of them. And so it goes.

But media people are just like people in other lines of work. They have diverse personalities, moods, values, ideas, and good and bad days, too. So when you first encounter a media type, whether by phone or in person, do the exercise where you learned to "smell your audience," where you tuned into where they might be coming from. It should be easier in this instance because you're dealing with only one individual. Be attentive from the very first hello to what your instincts are telling you, and go with them. It's part of that same sense improv actors get about their audiences when they first hit the stage. They take the audience in, assess them, and then go from there. All the previous chapters you've read and all the exercises you've practiced are really going to come into play now. This is definitely one of those times when the improv skills you've learned are going to be vitally important.

In your first encounter with your interviewers, try to meet them on their level. Are they friendly? Quiet? Uncertain? Dogmatic? Arrogant? Where are they coming from? Now, figure out what adjustments you need to make. You'll recall that most of the time your audience — in this case, the interviewers — will mirror you. If they detect the least bit of resistance or a defensive posture, they'll probably hit you over the head with it sooner or later during the interview. On the other hand, if you're pleasant, kind, poised, and so on, they'll probably respond in a more positive way. (Remember, it's very difficult to resist positive energy.) But keep your cool, no matter what happens.

If you start off being pleasant and poised, your interviewers probably will, too. And that being the case, your interview has a good chance of going your way, which usually means that you'll be able to tell your story the way you want people to hear it or read it. Never start out with any hint of hostility, even if you're being interviewed about a controversial subject, and the reporter is a jerk. (And the media does have its share of those, too, just like any other profession.) Keep in mind what I said at the beginning of the chapter: Media types are people, too, and will react and respond like most people in most situations. If you stay centered and calm, then the most obnoxious reporter can't get to you. But keep in mind that most of the time, reporters are simply out to get their stories — to get the facts. The way you present those facts at the outset of the interview may well determine the nature of the subsequent questions you're asked. You want those questions to be precursors for all the great things *you* want to say, whether you're making information points, or stating your side of a controversial issue.

If you can find out prior to the interview what type of questions you'll be asked, do so. The more prepared you are, the better. Sometimes the interviewers will pass that information on to your secretary or publicist, if you ask for it ahead of time. You can let them know, through your liaison, that you simply want to give them the best interview possible, and that there might be statistics or facts you'll need to research prior to the interview. Most importantly, planning ahead allows you to gain insight into where the reporter is coming from, and whether the story is going to feature you in a positive or negative light. If the interviewers refuse to provide you with any advance information, that in itself may be an indication that they're planning to put you on the hot seat or give you a difficult time. They may also hope to catch you off guard. If that happens, at least you'll have time to prepare for the worst, or even to decide not to grant the interview.

Most of the time — in fact, the majority of the time — reporters will let you know in advance the slant of the story they're after, or the crux of the material they wish to cover. Obviously, this will make you *feel* more comfortable, since you'll have the opportunity to concentrate on what *they* want and be able to provide it to them. It also gives you time to think about your answers and time to rehearse them. This is especially helpful if the subject matter is delicate or controversial. The more time you have to prepare, the better. After all, you'd do the same if you were preparing for a challenging role on stage. (Remember the "Miller" premise that everyone is a performer.) Always keep in mind that the outcome of that print magazine, newspaper story, or radio or television spot will be a historical event, recorded for all time; so the way you handle yourself can impact you, positively or negatively, for a long time to come.

I've had clients who impulsively made wisecracks or gave personal opinions that came back to haunt them for months, even years afterwards. If you keep in mind that it's *your* image at stake, you're likely to be more careful about *what* you say. Although you probably don't think of yourself as a celebrity, in a sense you are, at least for that moment in time that you're being interviewed. I know many publicists who worry daily about their clients, and what they might say to the press that could be counterproductive to the publicists' efforts to put their clients in a good light. A prime example is the elite group of press agents who handle television and film stars; they're constantly on guard, because one wrong comment and all hell could break loose. Such was the case with John Lennon when he flippantly declared that the Beatles were more popular than Jesus

Christ. You recall the negative impact that had, for a long, long time. I know some publicists who are hired simply to keep their clients' names *OUT* of the press at all times, and/or to keep their clients from being interviewed, for fear that these clients will jeopardize their careers.

Most business professionals can become celebrities in their own circles (it's all relative), and the end result of specific interviews can make or break them, too. Remember at all times that you want press, but only good press. Favorable publicity can further your goals, position you as an expert, help you sell your product, and ultimately build the image you want and need. Continual good publicity can generate more interviews and stories, thus maximizing your exposure. But, then, so can bad publicity. Once you hurt yourself with the media, it's a long road back.

Just like professional performers, you want good reviews. So during your interviews, be sure to watch both WHAT YOU SAY and HOW YOU SAY IT. Maintain your stage presence; don't break. Get in "character" and stay there. "Smell" your audience. Keep your concentration and awareness levels sharp and constant from the beginning of the interview through to the end. Stay in "sync" with yourself. If you do, your timing and spontaneity will be as close to perfection as human nature will permit. Use your self-expression techniques as you converse; they will help you throughout the interview to emphasize the points you're trying to make. Keep telling yourself you're going to be the best that you can be; that this is a grand performance, and you're going to "break a leg." Never forget that you're a performer, and every performance you give should be your best.

The following are some further suggestions, as well as some dos and don'ts, for handling the media:

1. Listen carefully to the question and answer it directly. Sometimes we hear questions subjectively and selectively, and answer accordingly. Instead, try to listen to the information from the point of view of the questioner. "Know" your audience and play to them.

2. Think about answering questions in terms of soundbites; that is, give your answers succinctly and incisively. Why?

Because if your interview is being pretaped, it might be edited. This happens on news programs all the time. So if you answer the question precisely up front and first, and then the interviewer cuts you off, you'll already have addressed what you think is the most important information, and you'll have said what needed to be said. Business professionals often exhibit a tendency to "lead" into their answers, and take forever to get to the *real* answer. You can't do this with the media. Remember, print and electronic media (particularly the latter) are designed to move quickly through their stories, from beginning to end. On television news, for instance, the longest story often takes up no more than two minutes. Feature segments may be longer; for example, you might have a 30-minute television interview or an extensive interview in a magazine or newspaper. But even in those circumstances it's imperative that you "get to the car crash" — in other words, answer that question! This strategy leaves time for more questions, more answers and, in the end, more exposure for the points you're trying to cover. My advice: Save the lengthy discussions for more appropriate venues, such as negotiating sessions and meetings.

3. Don't be defensive. When being interviewed by the media, people often have their guard up from the beginning. Remember your acting tips — particularly the fact that your "audience" will mirror you. Sometimes this mirroring is subtle or unconscious; sometimes it's blatant. If you start out the interview with even a hint of a defensive posture, you can get into big trouble. And once that ball is rolling, it can go straight downhill quickly. Be direct and firm, but kind and patient also. If you have to bring out the guns, bring them out only when you need to. The self-defense theory goes like this: If you start out defensive and guarded, the listener will perceive you as being insecure or having something to hide, which only weakens your credibility. On the other hand, if you "take the stage" (interview) with confidence, poise, and a sense of personal power, your interviewer will respond more positively, and you'll get what you're after — great coverage.

4. Keep *reasonable* control. If you come on too strong, too defensive, too anything, your need for control will be overly obvious to your interviewer and audience. Stay confident, relaxed, assured, and assertive, but don't be aggressive.

5. Be personable when it's appropriate. Listen for the host's name, and then use it occasionally when answering the questions; for example, "I'm glad you asked that, Susan." You tend to establish a better rapport when you call the interviewer by name. Watch some of the sports and entertainment celebrities who grant interviews. Notice how they sometimes use the host's name. If you happen to be on a call-in show, pay attention to the caller's name, and address her or him by name, too.

6. **Never say anything that you don't want to see in print or hear on the air.** Remember, some members of the press will attempt to get you to talk "off the record." In addition, they might also edit your remarks, so that a phrase or remark that you shouldn't have uttered can prove disastrous and/or come back to haunt you later on.

7. Talk *to* your audience. Be careful that you don't come off sounding superior, condescending, or pedantic. Also, you'll want to make sure that you use words that your audience can understand. For example, if you continually use technical information without explaining it, your audience will grow increasingly resentful. Instead, think "Jane, Dick and Spot." This will help you to keep your replies simple and to the point. Remember, the interviewer is passing on to the public the information you've provided. What do you want the media to tell your audience?

8. Don't say it twice. We all have, at times, a tendency to be redundant. Just say it once. Ask yourself as you go along, "Is this new information?"

9. Let them work for it — don't feel that you have to fill all the "dead air" in an interview, whether print or electronic. Make the interviewer work for your answers. When you've fully answered each question, wait for the interviewer to ask another. Don't feel that you have to keep talking, unless it's

beneficial for *you* to do so. Many interviewees make the mistake of thinking that it's up to them to keep the interview alive; but that's the interviewer's job. Make the host work for it.

10. Don't be afraid to repeat the question if you need a moment to gather your thoughts, think through an answer, or assimilate the content of the question. Also, it's a good idea at times to repeat the question in order to make sure that you understand it. Sometimes interviewees answer a question based on what they *thought* they heard, which can be embarrassing and misleading.

11. Be aware of your body language, whether you're on camera or not. Make sure you sit up straight, keep good eye contact, with your body solid, and your gestures appropriate to your dialogue. Behave much the same way you would before an audience at a speech or presentation. Remember the suggestions for maximizing your facial features and vocal range and abilities during speeches and presentations. The same holds true in an interview. Often, the subtle messages you put out, whether good or bad, will influence the reporter, which in turn will affect the outcome of the story or spot. All of your mannerisms and idiosyncrasies speak for you. Since you want to present yourself at your best, be conscious of what your body language is saying. In acting terms, the advice would be: Don't lose your stage presence at any time.

12. Listen to your voice to make certain you're not speaking in a monotone. Remember, too, what you've learned about the importance of mood variance and self-expression. Try to keep this in mind, especially if you're on the radio. Since your listeners will have only the sound of your voice to go on, that's all the more reason to make your voice as interesting as you possibly can!

13. Remember some of the other "Miller" pointers, such as the importance of good diction. During electronic interviews, a stable breathing technique will be very important. Remember, too, what you learned about spontaneity, timing, and energy level. Warm up by utilizing your concentration exercises prior to each interview. Get "in character." Think about

the "part" that you're about to play. Count on the fact that the media can be either your friend or your foe. You can establish some very important contacts with the media, contacts that will be useful throughout your career. It's not unusual for media personnel to move from one job to another, so always treat them with respect and consideration. Last year's small-town reporter could be the editor of *The Wall Street Journal* some day in the future. My former husband, a very well-known southern California sports columnist and broadcaster, used to say that the media was the most powerful collection of people in the world. Sound survival technique dictates that you treat each of them with thoughtfulness and care. This doesn't mean that you can't be yourself — relaxed and human, truthful and real. It just means that the media is something you want to utilize to your advantage, rather than having it work against you and your public image.

"Good afternoon. I'm Miller — the killer — speaker!"

THE "MILLER" EPILOGUE

Well, you did it. You've jogged arduously up the many mountains and overcome the gut-wrenching obstacles of "Miller" boot camp. So if you didn't skip any chapters, congratulations; you've reached the finish line and earned your stripes! You're now armed and ready to take on any speechmaking challenge.

In summary, I want to remind you to: Breathe properly, pronounce every letter of every word, warm up those vocal chords (and the mouth, tongue and throat) with good vocalization; make eye contact; work out those facial muscles and practice that body language; plug into your own sense of timing, express yourself more fully, and most importantly of all, let go and be spontaneous! Remember: Don't think; just be. Go with the flow. Be authentic and genuine. Think about what you're like when you're talking to your best friend in the kitchen.

Listen to what's being said and what's left *unsaid*, and respond to the subtext (the unsaid). Be agile and tuned in enough to do so. Outline your speech or presentation, but don't try to memorize it word for word. Think the outline through, keep it "Jane, Dick and Spot," and be sure to incorporate humor and good storytelling. "Smell" your audience.

You must remember that you're like a classic character: you're unique unto yourself. No other person has the same col-

lection of attributes, personality traits, overall ensemble of qualities — in other words, no one else's communication DNA
matches yours. So I want you to enjoy leaving your very own
personal impression everywhere you go. Build a character if
you need to.

More than anything, though, it's my hope (and "Miller's,"
too) that by practicing and then implementing the lessons in
this book, you'll come to cherish every speaking moment; and
that the positive feedback you get (whether it's applause or a
sale) will give you a new-found sense of satisfaction and pride
in your ability to come across effectively. As you work out the
"Miller" way, you're only going to get better and better. So keep
doing it.

You're a performer now. Knock 'em dead!

ABOUT THE AUTHOR

A founding member of the world-famous L.A. Groundlings, Cherie Kerr is the founder, and since 1990, the Executive Producer and Artistic Director of the Orange County Crazies, a sketch and improvisational comedy troupe that performs three original satirical revues a year at its own theater in Santa Ana, California. Kerr also serves as the group's chief writer.

Kerr has taught improvisational comedy to actors for the past 23 years, and teaches other classes as well, including one on how to write sketch comedy. She has studied with some of the best improv and comedy teachers in the business, including Gary Austin, founder of the L.A. Groundlings, and a former member of the highly acclaimed group, the Committee; Michael Gellman, a director and teacher for The Second City, in Chicago; and Jeanie Berlin (an Academy Award nominee and Elaine May's daughter).

Kerr founded ExecuProv in 1983, and has provided classes and private coaching to hundreds of business professionals. Her clients include ARCO, GTE, *Self* Magazine, Nissan Motors, Mitsubishi, Delta Dental, PacifiCare, Bank One, Bank of America and Casio, to name but a few. She has also worked for a number of government agencies, such as the L.A. City Attorney's Office, the L.A. District Attorney's Office, and the County of Orange. She is currently a Continuing Legal Education Provider for the State Bar of California, and has served as that organization's official trainer of speakers for its Board of Governors.

A writer for more than 25 years, Kerr has owned an award-winning public relations firm; written, produced, and directed an original full-scale musical comedy; is a member of ASCAP; and has been recognized numerous times as an award-winning journalist and publicist. Kerr was named, along with Disney's Michael Eisner, as one of the "Top Ten Most Sensational People In Orange County" by *Orange Coast Magazine*.

Kerr is currently working on several additional books based on information from her other ExecuProv courses, including People Skills (for one-on-one communication); Humor In The Workplace (how to stay lighter on the job); and What's So Funny? (how to get humor into your speeches and presentations).

In addition to lecturing and teaching ExecuProv, both in classroom situations and in private, one-on-one tutoring sessions, Kerr provides speechwriting services for many of her clients.

Her three children and grandson are the most important part of her life.

ExecuProv offers workshop sessions, seminars and private coaching to both companies and individuals world wide. Ms. Kerr is available for keynote speeches and special appearances. Please submit a written request for any of the above to:

ExecuProv
P.O. Box 4444
Santa Ana, CA 92701-4444

Other Books by Cherie Kerr available in 1996:

What's So Funny — How to get good story telling and humor into your speeches and presentations

When I Say This... Do You Mean That? — People skills and one-on-one communications techniques

Humor in the Workplace and Every Other Place — Keeping humor and levity in your workday and every day

How to Think Fast on Your Feet Without Putting Them in Your Mouth — The how-to's of being and staying spontaneous

— — — — — — — — — — — — — — — — — — —

I would like to order the following books:

___ copies of *What's So Funny*

___ copies of *When I Say This...*

___ copies of *Humor in the Workplace...*

___ copies of *How to Think Fast on Your Feet...*

Name _____

Address _____

City_____

State _____ Zip _____

Telephone No._____ Fax No. _____

Credit Card ❑ Visa ❑ MasterCard

Credit Card No. _____

Expiration Date _____

Signature _____

If you would like additional information on the above books, please call (714) 550-9900 or write to ExecuProv, P.O. Box 4444, Santa Ana, CA 92701. Please mail order forms to the same address.